INTRACOASTAL VOYAGE OF THE SEA SCAPE

CAPTAIN RAMI GEFFNER, MD
C.W. BRANCO

ISBN 979-8-9915999-0-0 (paperback)

ISBN 979-8-9915999-1-7 (ebook)

Cover design and Interior formatting by Aaxel Author Group

 www.aaxelauthorgroup.com

To my parents, Sara & Herb Geffner

"Every pole has two ends!"
—my father's favorite proverb

Thank you for your love and for giving me the vision, support, strength, and confidence needed to examine both ends and find the right decision for myself.

Rami

To my husband, Bob

My journey with you is the best journey of all!

Cath

DISCLAIMER

Included here is a disclaimer taken from work by Robert Sherer, another captain who travels the Atlantic Ocean and the Atlantic Intracoastal Waterway and writes about it:

"It is important for all my readers to know that before partaking in this book you are agreeing to the following:

In no event shall Rami Geffner or C. W. Branco, the co-authors or their entities, be liable for any direct, indirect, incidental, special exemplary, or consequential damages (including, but not limited to, procurement of substitute goods or services: loss of use, data, or profits; or business interruptions) however caused and on any theory of liability, whether in contract, strict liability, or tort (including negligence or otherwise) arising in any way out of the use of this book or its product, even if advised of the possibility of such damage. This limitation shall apply to claims of personal injury to the extent permitted by law.

This book is to be considered an aid for leisure navigation. It can contain errors and cannot substitute for the official government charts. Only official government charts and notices to mariners contain all the information needed for safe navigation. The charts in this book are derived from MapQuest, Marinas.com, Mapcarta. com, and Google, which can contain inaccuracies and may not contain the latest updates. It is the user's responsibility to use this information prudently.

This book or its charts does not meet the carriage requirements for the Coast Guard. They are derived from MapQuest, Marinas.com, Mapcarta.com, and Google. Which are not the strict standards required to satisfy the carriage requirement. See Title 33 CFR, Part 164 for details.

The main reason for the above disclaimer is the changing nature of the ICW. What worked yesterday may not work the next day due to tides, currents, wind, wave action, or any other undeterminable changes in land or waterways. Of course, through my own experience and through the experiences of others to whom will correspond with the author any notable experiences will be noted in any additions to future volumes."

CONTENTS

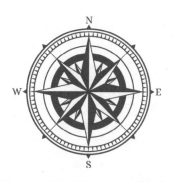

DOCKING SITES

Day #	Date	Heading to	Marina
Home Base	Home Dock	Tuckahoe River, New Jersey	Yank Marina
Day 1	11/5/22	Chincoteague, Virginia	Robert N. Reed Waterfront Park
Day 2	11/6/22	Norfolk, Virginia	Waterside Marina
Day 3	11/7/22	Columbia, North Carolina	Alligator River Marina
Day 4	11/8/22	Morehead City, North Carolina	Portside Marina
Day 5	11/9/22	Wilmington, North Carolina	Bridge Tender Marina
Day 6	11/10/22	North Myrtle Beach, North Carolina	Harbourgate Marina
Day 7	11/11/22	Georgetown, South Carolina	Harborwalk Marina
Day 8	11/12/22	Charleston, South Carolina	Ripley Light Marina
Day 9	11/13/22	Beaufort, South Carolina	Safe Harbor Port Royal Marina

Day #	Date	Heading to	Marina
Day 10	11/14/22	Darien, Georgia	Darien River – A Free Dock
Day 11	11/15/22	Jacksonville, Florida	Windward Beach Marina
Day 12	11/16/22	Port Canaveral, Florida	Bluepoints Marina
Day 13	11/17/22	Fort Pierce, Florida	Fort Pierce City Marina
Day 14	11/18/22	Fort Lauderdale, Florida	Home-Sweet-Home

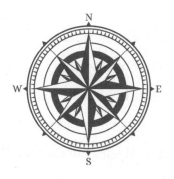

PREFACE

My passion for the sea started when I was a young boy growing up in Israel. My parents moved to Brooklyn, New York, when I was nine years old, and along with my luggage, I brought my love of the sea. Again, we lived not far from the sea, and again, I was able to feed my passion for the ocean. As soon as I was able, I bought my first boat. As my passion grew, so did the size of my boats. I slowly built up to the purchase of my Horizon PC60 power catamaran vessel in 2021, which I named the *Sea Scape*.

Prior to my purchase of the *Sea Scape* I had a good understanding of how boats worked and how to operate them. I had picked up my knowledge from my many boating friends who generously shared their knowledge, answered my questions, and gave me some of their tips. But the *Sea Scape* was a much bigger boat than any I had owned. I knew it could take me places I had not ventured before. I bought the *Sea Scape* not only to enjoy the sea but also to indulge my passion for deep-sea fishing.

After buying that catamaran, I knew I needed to bolster my knowledge even further. My first concern was how to drive the boat properly. The other boats I owned were small enough so that I was able to see from all sides. The *Sea Scape*'s size and design did not have that advantage, so I knew operating that boat would be very different and more complex. Secondly, I wanted to gain a fuller understanding of the *Sea Scape*'s mechanics in case of an emergency. If only for the issue of safety, I needed to be able to troubleshoot the most essential things. Plus, I wanted to know all I could about this boat!

I had a lot of "unofficial knowledge" but no official captain's license. Therefore I decided that was the first place to start. Getting the license was a formidable task requiring an enormous amount of studying. I found it informative and enlightening and learned a lot about boat operation and how the sea could affect a boat's operation. Then, to add to my understanding of the mechanics, I sought information by asking questions of several professional marine mechanics I knew. My reasons were twofold: I knew I wouldn't be able to enjoy my boat if I could not operate it correctly, and the second reason had to do with my insurance company.

According to my insurance company, hurricane season

determined the boat's location. If I were to keep the boat in New Jersey year-round, I would need to winterize it and put it into storage. With this need in mind, I decided to dock the boat in New Jersey in the summer and then move it to Fort Lauderdale, Florida, to use during the winter months. This satisfied my insurance company's regulation. Thus, I committed to a trip from New Jersey to Florida and Florida to New Jersey each year.

On my first trip moving the boat from Florida to New Jersey, I hired a captain, thinking he would teach me all I needed. Unfortunately, he proved disappointing. He did not have the capacity or patience for the job. I would ask about charts, the route, or maneuvering the boat, and he would often tell me to just watch or look at the chart and tell him what I saw. He would never take the time to fully answer my questions. He once even asked if I was ever going to stop asking him questions! Unbelievable! His lack of patience and unwillingness to share information made him a poor choice and certainly left a foul taste in my mouth! If I ever need a "teacher" again, I will certainly take the time beforehand to find out the person's willingness to share and teach.

After that experience, I knew I would have to train myself as much as possible. Preparing for my second voyage in the fall of 2022, I educated myself for my first big trip from New Jersey to Fort Lauderdale, Florida. I scoured both the internet and bookstores and found many that offered plenty of information, along with great navigational details. Still, I was not looking for any great detail on the subject yet, only simple references such as how long I should plan to travel each day, which rivers or creeks were part of the Intracoastal and which to follow, which shortcuts were advisable and which could be dangerous, which were the best marinas to use, and which had fuel, along with many other general concerns. This information was nowhere to be concisely found. All I wanted and needed was one book to take me down the entire route. Even if there were other directions my path to knowledge could take me, I was looking for one main route from which to start.

I studied the Intracoastal Waterway and used every navigational tool I had. At that time in my life, I wish I could have initially found what I later created in this book: a passage delineating the route and a clear, simple reference for traveling the Intracoastal Waterways to use as a starting point for planning a safe voyage. I realized that I could turn to other sources with greater navigational summaries if I needed more details. I also realized that others might need such a starting point as well.

I once spoke with a guy who told me how he would have loved to have taken his boat to Florida but just did not know where to start. This book provides just that, offering a general route, zooming in on specific areas, providing maps, noting warnings and alerts, and covering some historical details of areas we passed. I wanted to create a resource that the typical boater would easily read while in the comfort of their recliner—a formidable recall of worthwhile information that could aid anyone traveling the Intracoastal Waterway. Keeping an account of the voyage, I knew, would later allow us to pass on what we learned from our day-to-day experiences. Much like building a house, it can help create the foundation for anyone's trip on the Intracoastal. I do not want the reader to underestimate the importance of other available resources, but I feel there is a need for both the general and the more detailed. So, I intend to give boaters such as the man who missed out on this trip to Florida a starting point. However, I also realize and would like to assert here that it is not until one knows their boat well and travels the Intracoastal Waterway a few times that one feels more comfortable with this journey.

In this book, we hope the reader will find the information they need to develop a great starting point or add to the knowledge they already possess. We welcome and thank all who wish to share any information and experiences that can support future volumes of this book and wish everyone an enjoyable and safe trip.

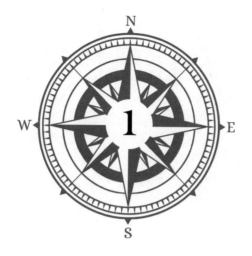

MEET THE *SEA SCAPE* AND ITS CAPTAIN!

"Believe me, my young friend, there is nothing - absolutely nothing - half so much worth doing as simply messing about in boats."

–*Kenneth Grahame*

Sea Scape

The *Sea Scape* is a 61'9-3/8" Horizon power catamaran, built in Taiwan with a 24.6 ft. beam and a maximum draught of 4.95 ft. It weighs 44 tons, has two C12 Caterpillar engines and one Onan generator that is 21.5 KW, and a second Onan generator that is 9 KW single phase, with 4 thrusters.

The *Sea Scape*'s pilot house, the nerve center of the boat, houses the highly sensitive computer system, which contains two Garmin monitors and an up-to-date, real-time warning detection system, designed to constantly monitor all the boat's critical systems. It is quartered in a sleek yet comfortable dashboard that can quickly alert the captain if there is the slightest problem with the engines or if any boat-related safety issues must be addressed.

A view from the *Sea Scape*'s striking galley, equipped with all the conveniences of a well-planned kitchen. Through the salon's double sliding glass doors, one can see the stern with its dining table and six chairs.

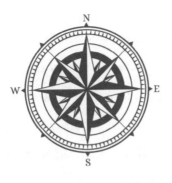

November, 2022

Whenever I look out at the sea I perceive it as a mystical place. Even as a child, I was not attracted to just the sea as a whole but all of its components, be it the early morning glint of the sun on the waves, helping change the sky's color to purple or pink; the sand forming and reforming at the edge of the shoreline in frothy, foaming trails; the billowy clouds allowing the sun to shine through and brighten the deep sapphire color of the ocean; or the imposing, ominous clouds, acting like nature's weatherman as they predicted gloomy, thick sheets of rain. Even as an adult, I can still become mesmerized by the motion of the waves as they form and then just as quickly disappear or when, at other times, they perform mother nature's dance in the moonlight or sing their song, sometimes lapping against the boat's side before I fall asleep or sounding like a big drum beating down in angry weather.

Sometimes what fascinates me most are the creatures that call the ocean home. I started my first serious adventure with the sea working as a research assistant at Sandy Hook, New Jersey's marine laboratory. I took the job because I had an interest in marine biology but did not continue with it because eventually, I realized that my salary expectations did not meet the level of education I would have needed to continue in this field. I therefore chose medicine, which led me to the field of dermatology.

One of the missions of the marine biology lab was to collect marine species and observe the effects of pollution, and as I stood at the shoreline, collecting specimens, I began to further appreciate the vastness and power of the ocean. Standing at the water's edge, I could look out and see New York City and the commercial and non-commercial traffic on the waterway. Big ships and little boats— it was a maritime highway with vessels coming and going from all around the world! I liked to try to imagine where they came from, what they were doing, and where they would go after they left New York. I imagined myself on one of the smaller non-commercial boats weaving between the vessels so I could get a closer look! But alas, I always had to return to my work at hand!

At that time, waste was being dumped into the New York Harbor about twenty miles offshore, and marine life was beginning to show the effects. The consequences of this still poke at my intellect, which served to further my fascination with the ocean and all its magnificence. I would look at its deep, midnight-blue hue and feel something pulling me. A spiritual, intellectual, and physical connection kept calling me back, a feeling that would repeat throughout my life.

One person who furthered my interest in the sea was Dr. Wayne Draesel, an internist I met while serving as the dermatologist on call at Toms River Community Medical Center in Toms River, New Jersey. After referring several patients to me, we began to engage in some noteworthy conversations about the sea in which we both had an interest. One day he invited me to join him for a day of boating and fishing on his 21 foot Grady White Cuddy cabin boat. This was my first introduction to having sea spray salt hit my face while we whipped through the water, and I found it captivating except for one thing. It introduced me to another hindrance associated with the ocean. I was marred with the dreaded villain of first-time sailors: seasickness. It took me ten years of continuous persistence to overcome this demon. But I was determined and finally, my body and mind acclimated. I ultimately developed strong sea legs and became even more passionate about cruising and fishing.

The trip unveiled in these pages is meant to entice and captivate but more importantly assist anyone planning a trip down the United States' Northeast shoreline using the Intracoastal Waterway. After making my first trip to Florida, I knew I would need to share my experience so others could gain from my insights. This book is as much about what one can and should do as it is about becoming aware of not to do. By the time I reached my destination, I had bent the propellers and shaft and had a few other problems, including clogged fuel filters, a scratched fiberglass hull, and water filters that required cleaning due to an abundant buildup of debris. Needless to say, those repairs were not only incredibly expensive but also incredibly time-consuming. I hope that my insights can save you time and money and make your trip more enjoyable!

My decision to invest in a Horizon PC60 catamaran came after years of research and involved enormous trial and error. The design features of the Horizon Catamaran PC 60 had a major impact on me when I considered buying the *Sea Scape*. It has two diesel engines and a thirteen-hundred-gallon fuel capacity, allowing for reasonable travel before refueling. Traveling at a speed of seven to eight knots, the *Sea Scape* burns about eight to nine gallons an hour, and at around twenty knots, approximately fifty to sixty gallons an hour. One excellent feature of the *Sea Scape* is an inside connecting staircase between the main salon located on the second floor and the pilothouse on the third floor. The Anigre wood staircase is commonly used for high-end interior furniture and cabinetry and was used on board for much of the boat's interior decor. This internal staircase creates a passage between the second and third floors to the pilothouse. Many other boats force you to leave the protection of cover and face the elements to move between floors; this was not the case with the *Sea Scape*'s design.

When the weather is inclement, the staircase provides an easy passage between the two levels, allowing passengers to move safely from the salon to the pilot house. Food and drinks, dirty dishes, books, a change of clothing, a warm sweater, or any additional gear, if needed, can be brought up or down to a level during harsh weather without encountering cold rain or blustery, gusting winds, eliminating the potential for rain slapping you in the face or wind blowing things out of your hands! It is like having a home with an attached garage so you do not have to battle the outside elements. What a bonus!

The only addition I would have liked would have been more amenities for deep-sea fishing. So, after careful consideration of all the boat had to offer compared to others, I decided I could add the things needed for deep-sea fishing and thus, decided this was the boat for me.

Because of all the boat's positives, I only had to make a few additions to enhance the fishing experience. First on my list was a Frigibar, a top-of-the-line powerful marine ice maker. This machine takes care of all my needs. It was a great addition! Hey, you have to keep the fish you catch on ice! I next added two fighting stands, one on each rear pontoon. Each stand allows an angler to strap themselves into a harness on the stand while at the boat's edge.

Additionally, it allows for the placement of the butt of the fishing pole into a rod butt holder while fighting the fish. The stand swivels 180 degrees.

Auxiliary rod holders on the stern gunnel enhance the ease of the fishing experience by increasing the number of rod holders from four to eight. These rod holders help increase the chance of getting a bite-on. On the stern deck behind the pilot house is a six-foot chest freezer holding twenty cubic feet of storage, primarily intended for fish and bait to support the fishing experience.

Next, on the main aft level, I had a supplementary Garmin plotter, charter, and radar installed, which connects to the pilothouse instrumentation for use while on this level. The installation of nine outside cameras allows viewing of everything around the boat on a single monitor, especially while trolling at the stern while in the ocean when no other boats are around.

Outside bar lights, installed on each side of the pilothouse, illuminate all sides of the boat in darkness. For our listening pleasure, a new sound system provides astonishing surround sound throughout the boat. Communication is particularly important to me, so I had a true satellite phone installed. We can communicate with anybody, anywhere in the world, as long as the satellite in the sky is in motion. It provides a connection as clear as a bell!

The stern of the boat has its own driving station (green arrow), which has a Garmin monitor (red arrow) above it. Any desired screen can be selected for view. In addition, a monitor (yellow arrow) displays 9 camera feeds, providing views of the bow, port, and starboard sides.

Every boat owner knows that thrusters move a boat sideways, making it much easier to maneuver than just by the engine's propellers. Standing in the pilothouse, one cannot see the stern or either side of the boat. Using only the thrusters, I would have to depend on my first mate to be in the areas I could not see. My first mate, wearing wireless mounting headphones, can transmit the information needed whenever moving the boat using the thrusters. Without additional thrusters, such maneuvering would be laborious, stressful, time-consuming, and, in some cases, depending on the wind, a tricky process.

I once met a boat captain who told me sufficient thruster power would make driving a boat this size much more enjoyable and manageable. He had driven a boat with four thrusters, he told me, and maneuvering it was a dream! That made sense to me—making it easier to maneuver the boat also made it safer for the vessel and those on board. So, following that old skipper's advice, I added three more thrusters for a total of four, which proved to be a luxury and well-thought-out addition to improving maneuverability. The *Sea Scape* was one of my life's dreams, and I knew these thrusters would make this boat extremely seaworthy. So, I made it happen!

I also invested in an onboard video system with eight cameras for a complete surrounding view. These cameras can see the bow, stern, port, and starboard. The screens that display these camera views can be seen both in the pilothouse and the stern of the boat, thus allowing for easy access and viewing of all surrounding sides.

By the end of the trip, I also realized my experiences over the past forty years were not insignificant and were worth it. Otherwise, I would not have known what I really and truly needed, and putting all these additions to the test was money well spent. My wife, Patty, says, "Experience is what you get when you don't get what you want." As many cruisers and fishermen would attest, all the above knowledge takes time to cultivate. It is essential to understand that knowledge and wisdom develop as a process over time, multiplied by expertise. The years before bestowed me with knowledge and imparted me with wisdom. My *Sea Scape* is the culmination of my experiences with other boats and my knowledge of what is needed for deep-sea fishing. My efforts to customize and tailor it to my needs have only added to the efficiency and my enjoyment of this wonderful vessel!

FIRST THINGS FIRST

"Luck is when preparation meets opportunity."

—Seneca the Younger, philosopher of ancient Rome

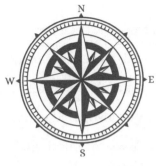

November, 2022

Yank Marina
Tuckahoe, New Jersey

My *Sea Scape* was docked at the hard-working Yank Marina in Tuckahoe, New Jersey. They have over fifty years of experience building and refurbishing all types of boats—including private yachts, commercial boats, and even military vessels—and are proficient in working with wood, fiberglass, steel, and aluminum, and can lift vessels up to three hundred metric tons. One of the main reasons I decided to use them is because they can accommodate a boat as wide as the *Sea Scape* and more importantly, have a Marine Travelift that can lift 820 metric/903 US-ton vessels. They are a serious marina and do seriously good work.

While trying to make the most distance each day, it became difficult for me to judge the approximate time and place to book a dock to cover the maximum cruising time. Two problems regarding this trip were evident from the beginning. One was the docking of the *Sea Scape*. There needs to be more marinas to choose from for docking such a wide yacht. A friend told me that many marinas built in the past were not constructed with consideration for wider boats, such as the *Sea Scape*, in mind, mainly because there were simply fewer catamaran yachts in those days. The problem with docking the *Sea Scape*, a powered catamaran with a twenty-five-foot-wide beam, is that it would only fit at a tee dock, meaning the end of a pier; a bulkhead dock; or a fuel dock. Typically, one would try to reserve an overnight docking in advance to ensure a specific type of slip. Most marinas allow for a two-to-three-day advanced reservation. My desire to make good time and distance would be stalled if the trip became contingent on a dock reservation made too far in advance.

Navionics was the key to solving my docking dilemma and has proven to be my most trusted reference for booking a dock. Not only did it provide dock-to-dock route guidance, but it also identified precautions for shallow water and hazards, aided in estimating fuel consumption, gave estimated times of arrival to a specific marina, and even allowed me to identify a variety of marinas close to my location while making our way through the Intracoastal Waterway. The system lists the marinas alphabetically, providing their phone numbers and information on their ability to refuel, food accessibility, nearby sights, restaurants, bars, shops, and accessible repair dealers, all updated daily. I planned to use the information from the Navionics system to begin contacting marinas about three hours before desiring to dock and then make a reservation closer to my actual arrival time. Most of the time, I could use my cell phone to call 99 percent of all the marinas to find a suitable slip for that day. Occasionally, I had to use my satellite phone system. Unfortunately, our choice of overnight docking space was limited because there was hardly enough of the type of dock space that we required and because we did not have a prior reservation. However, we could still use the Navionics for our daily planning and to find a private marina for docking space for two days out of the trip. We consider ourselves very lucky!

Most marinas have fuel stations, so refueling was not a significant concern. The *Sea Scape* holds thirteen hundred gallons of fuel, and I calculated that the most we would use came close to six hundred gallons a day between both engines. Never knowing where our next fueling station would be or what difficulties we could run into, I planned to refuel at every marina we docked at, no matter the price, because I wanted to avoid being short of fuel at any time. Being short of fuel means having to wait for help, and no one knows how long that might take. Running out of fuel can become a very dangerous thing. The boat has a generator that supplies the electricity for the air-conditioning, the kitchen and appliances, and many other necessities. But the most important thing not to lose control of is the desalinating machine. If you run out of drinkable water, you are in big trouble! You can switch from the generator to the batteries, but that would only last for eight to ten hours. Then you're speaking about real distress!

I always felt that being fully fueled took first priority. Docking at the fuel station became our preference because it not only eliminated moving the boat around the marina twice but also took care of getting a slip that was wide enough. If the *Sea Scape* was allowed to stay at a marina's fuel dock, she had to leave early the following day, which we always planned for, so that was not a problem. It also made it easy to fill up with fuel. We also realized that we would most likely be the last in and needed to be the first out, but that worked for us.

Another consideration at the time of planning was that I needed to figure out whether I could navigate the entire course on the Atlantic Ocean. Between New Jersey and Norfolk, Virginia, there is no passage on the Intracoastal Waterway (ICW). I knew I had to use the Atlantic Ocean for this location. We also knew that when the weather changed, the Intracoastal Waterway would provide us with a safer path. However, due to the large area of no wake along the Intracoastal Waterway, our decreased speed would make the trip longer. As I researched, I learned I needed to use the Atlantic Ocean for two days going from New Jersey to Chincoteague, Virginia, and again between Chincoteague and Norfolk, Virginia. Thus, we used the Atlantic Intracoastal Waterway for the remainder of the trip. After all that, we were ready to begin our journey.

Nonetheless, there is always something that eventually puts a kink in the plan. According to the books, hurricane season runs from June 1 to November 30, but not so for the insurance company. They allowed us to move the boat south of the Virginia border by October 31, which they consider the minimal risk time for hurricanes. Since weather can change swiftly, and safety always comes first, I always wanted to be prepared. Bad weather is the work of Mother Nature, and I do not battle with her! If bad weather were to occur, my decision has always been to allow Mother Nature to have her way and to keep the *Sea Scape* as safe as possible at a dock, seek shelter, and ride it out. Hurricane Ian made landfall on September 23, 2022, near Vero Beach, Florida. I planned to leave on November 5, forty-four days after Ian hit to ensure that the hurricane would no longer be a concern. Though, when we left, I knew that we were still at the tail end of hurricane season, the probability of another hurricane this late in the season seemed rare. Still, one can never be too prepared.

With this in the back of my mind, I knew it was important to listen and watch for accurate weather reports. I had accomplished my planning, and we were now ready to set sail.

OUR VOYAGE BEGINS

"The difference between a fairy tale and a sea tale? A fairy tale starts with 'Once upon a time.' A sea tale starts with 'This ain't no shit!'"

—*Edith Widder*

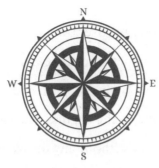

November 5, 2022

Yank Marina, Tuckahoe, NJ
- To -
Robert N. Reed Waterfront Park Marina,
Chincoteague, VA

Saturday, November 5, 2022, welcomed partly cloudy skies with a morning temperature nearing sixty degrees and heading to the mid-seventies by the afternoon. My first mate, Lauri, and I woke up early after spending the night on the *Sea Scape*, docked at the Yank Marina, Tuckahoe, New Jersey. The first leg of this voyage led us down the Tuckahoe River to the Great Egg Harbor Bay and then through Little Egg Harbor Inlet out to the brilliant Atlantic Ocean. We planned to travel between fifty and ninety miles a day, depending on cruising conditions. We knew that if all went well, this would bring us to our first docking site, Chincoteague, Virginia, about eighty-eight miles away.

True adventures come with surprises, and this story is no exception. Every boat owner wants to be ready for any problems that might make the ride an adventure! If something can go wrong, it will. I started the engines, and there it was—our first problem! The alarm sounded on both our port and starboard Caterpillar C12 engines. Next, one of the engines shut down and stalled, but we were able to restart it without any problems. I put out a call to a Caterpillar mechanic I knew who worked for Foley Equipment. After a lengthy discussion, the mechanic told me as long as the boat appeared to be functioning well, we could proceed. If the alarms kept sounding, we could take care of it along the way if needed or at our destination. He advised me to ignore the alarm and shut it off whenever it came back on, so off we went. I explained to him we were stressed about time because it was already late in the season, and we needed to get started on the long journey ahead of us. That was why he assured us that if the engines seemed to be working okay, we could keep moving despite the alarms. Perhaps, he went on, it was just a bad sensor. So off we went hoping he was correct and that there would be no problem. Imagine that!

The first part of our journey took us down the noteworthy Tuckahoe River, one of the few backwater rivers in the Northeastern United States. A river with little or no current, the Tuckahoe draws from the New Jersey Pinelands and empties into the Great Egg Harbor Bay, a passage into the Atlantic Ocean.

The Great Egg Harbor Bay, an estuary surrounded by backwater marshland, has unmatched beauty. An estuary is a partially enclosed body of brackish water with more salinity than freshwater but not as much as saltwater. The land often found at the edges of such estuaries is virtually treeless with an abundance of marsh grasses, better known as reeds. Their plant roots bind to the soil and slow the water flow. Their smooth stems and feathery tops sway in the wind and form a wave, like the folds in a flag or the swaying of two dancers. It was reminiscent of other places we had seen while traveling through the southern Intracoastal Waterways.

This splendid show of grasses waving in the wind continued down the long, curvy, snake-like Tuckahoe River as we coursed east to west, winding out into the Great Egg Harbor Bay and then on to the Atlantic Ocean for a total of twelve and a half nautical miles. This river was relatively shallow in many areas, so we needed to get up early that day to move the boat out on the high tide, which occurred in the early morning. Some days, you could see huge charter fishing boats maneuvering their way up the river, using escort boats to lead their way and prevent them from running aground.

There are some particularly shallow areas along the Tuckahoe River. The first part of this passage called for eyes wide open and knowledge of plotting our way around the shallow waters. Our powered catamaran, with its aforementioned twenty-five-foot beam, draws close to five feet of water, so we had to be very careful. When I purchased the boat, the Horizon Company told me the eye of the sonar depth finder lay at the very depth of the keel.

After our vigilant and calm trip down the Tuckahoe River, we entered the Great Egg Harbor Bay, which lies between Atlantic City, New Jersey, and Cape May, New Jersey. The 1619 Dutch explorer Cornelius Jacobson described it as an area plentiful in birds laying eggs. He named it Eyren Haven in Dutch, which translates to Egg Harbor.

The Tuckahoe River is one of seventeen tributaries, along with the Great Egg Harbor River, that feeds the 8.5-square-mile Great Egg Harbor Bay, passing under the New Jersey Garden State Parkway Bridge, the MacArthur Boulevard Bridge, and the Ocean City-Longport Bridge. Our trip so far, from Tuckahoe to the Great Egg Harbor Bay, had been short, taking only an hour and a half. We exited the bay at the Little Egg Inlet, which is one mile wide. If it was low tide, we would have had to watch out for any shoals.

Of the fourteen trustworthy New Jersey passages to the Atlantic Ocean, the Little Egg Inlet is one of the most reliable during the greater period of seasons in New Jersey. The great

Atlantic Ocean met us with its salty spray once we were through the inlet. I stood inside the pilothouse surrounded by five large glass panes of windows, and my passion for this magnificent blue water surrounded me. The waters sparkled like diamonds, and I could taste the ocean as I inhaled the salty air. The waves sang to me as the silent purr of the engines listened to my heart. It roused my memories and reignited my passion. Onward we went!

The *Sea Scape* entered the Atlantic Ocean and proceeded south toward Virginia's Chincoteague River to find our first night's haven. The ocean was calm, and we cruised at sixteen knots an hour after launching the boat at twenty knots an hour, with an RPM of 2,200 revolutions for just a little while so as not to stress our engines. We maintained a steady pace with clear weather predicted all the way to Virginia. My calculations estimated that in about five to six hours, after covering nearly one hundred nautical miles, we would arrive at Chincoteague, Virginia.

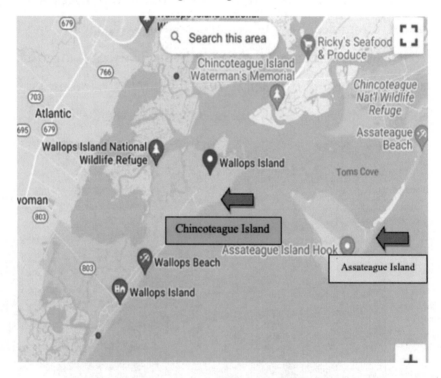

I used my Navionics to search for a marina as we approached Chincoteague Island, and I spoke to a marina manager and explained the *Sea Scape*'s requirements using my satellite phone. The marina manager immediately pointed me toward the Robert Reed Waterfront Park free dock, noting that this marina would be most able to accommodate us. After entering the Chincoteague Inlet, we traveled a couple of miles west. The Chincoteague free dock was quiet, with no amenities except a restroom. There were no electric hookups or fuel available anywhere, at least none that we could determine that evening.

The *Sea Scape*, harbored along the bulkhead pier of the free dock at Robert Reed Waterfront Park in Chincoteague, Virginia November 5, 2022

After docking, we had about an hour before everything closed down. The free dock is in the downtown area and within a couple of walking blocks from restaurants and souvenir shops, so we left the dock on foot. We explored a shop close to the pier, bought a couple of presents for the family, then returned to the boat and called it a night.

Without any electrical hookup, we slept with our night generator on. The *Sea Scape* is a relatively quiet boat built with thick foam and fiberglass. We could barely hear the generators, which are enclosed and located in the hull of the engine compartment, thus allowing for a restful sleep that night. Since our primary intent was to get to Florida safely and on time, we did not stop to see the local attractions the following day, though we imagined that they would have been very engaging. If we had the time, there was certainly a lot to explore. The first day of our journey held no real surprises.

One of the most magnificent sights in this area is the wild ponies, made famous in the novel *Misty of Chincoteague* by Marguerite Henry. Only twelve locations in North America remain where you can see wild ponies: out west in North Dakota, Colorado, Nevada, Arizona, Utah, Montana, Wyoming, Oregon, and along the Eastern Seaboard in Chincoteague/Assateague; the Outer Banks of North Carolina; Cumberland Island, Georgia; and Nova Scotia, Canada.

Chincoteague sits between Virginia and Maryland. The Virginia side of the island is home to Virginia's wild ponies at the Chincoteague National Wildlife Refuge. The Chincoteague Volunteer Fire Company has a permit for 150 adult ponies and privately owns and manages the herd. The Assateague Island National Seashore, located in Maryland, is also home to wild ponies and is governed by the National Park Service. One of their most prominent tourist attractions occurs every July when the

Chincoteague Volunteer Fire Company's Saltwater Cowboys bring the herd from Assateague Island to Chincoteague Island to auction off the excess ponies. Year 2022 set a record-breaking sale price of $7,146 for a single pony. The money collected helps support the fire department and provide veterinarian care for the ponies.

Florida is not the only place to see rockets launched into space! Another attraction in the area is Wallops Island and its magnificent connection to NASA's Wallops Flight Facility. Wallops Island, in partnership with the U.S. Navy National Oceanic and Atmospheric Administration and Federal Aviation Administration, is the test site for research aircraft, unmanned aerial systems, high-altitude balloons, and suborbital rockets. They are also open for tours daily, and on many days, one can witness rocket launches from their site. Visit the Wallops Visitor Center at their website, https://www.nasa.gov/wallops/visitor-center/, to find out their launch schedule for the day you stop over. Once a month, model rocket enthusiasts can launch their own rockets from a launch pad set up on the site.

We wish we could have stayed longer. It certainly proved a place to add to our bucket list of areas to spend more time in; maybe next year, we will return to visit the ponies! The following day at 6 a.m., we untied our lines and proceeded out the Chincoteague to reenter the Atlantic Ocean and make way to Norfolk, Virginia, continuing our journey south for the second day of our journey.

OVERVIEW

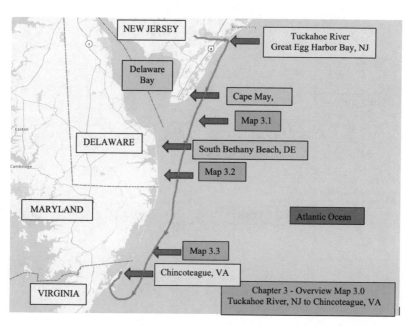

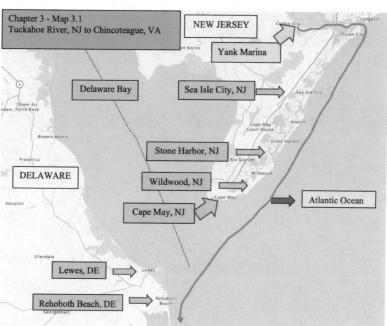

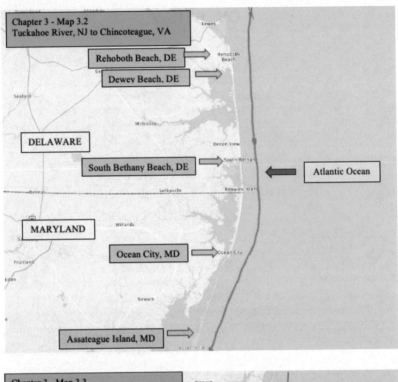

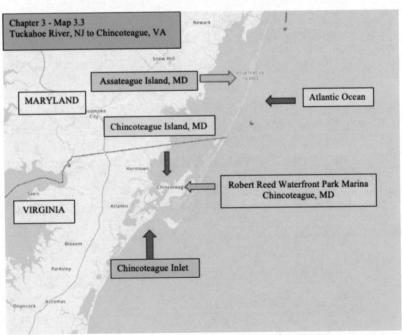

FINGER LICKIN' GOOD!

"Ships at a distance have every
man's wish on board."

–Zora Neale Hurston

November 6, 2022

Robert N. Reed Waterfront Park Free Marina
Chincoteague, Virginia
To
Waterside Marina, Norfolk, Virginia

We left Chincoteague about 8:30 the next morning, the start of a beautiful, sunlit day, and headed south around the Chincoteague Natural Wildlife Refuge out to the Atlantic Ocean. The Ocean was flat and glistening as we headed down the Delmarva Peninsula toward the Chesapeake Bay to our next destination, Norfolk, Virginia, about one hundred nautical miles away, where we planned to meet up with my friend Captain Mike and his first mate, Alex. I met Captain Mike at the Fort Lauderdale International Boat Show. Captain Mike is a professional captain who transports boats over the entire world. He was delivering *The Matrix*, a thirty-six-foot catamaran boat from Rochester, New York, to Fort Lauderdale, Florida.

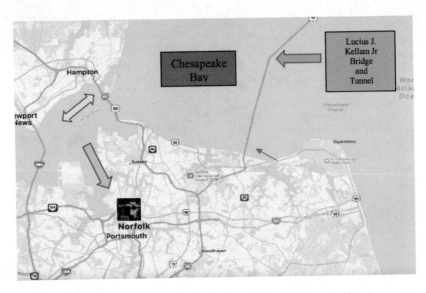

The Chesapeake Bay (red label) leads to Norfolk through Hampton Roads (yellow arrow) and then southeast on the Elizabeth River (green arrow). The river courses south and divides into an eastern branch, which goes to the Albemarle and Chesapeake Canal and a western route called the Deep Creek canal.

Fort Lauderdale, the "Yachting Capital of the World," has three hundred miles of inland waterways and is home to over fifty thousand boats. Over two thousand mega-yachts visit its waterways yearly, and every leading marine manufacturer has an office within this city. Although other cities have tried to outmatch it, the Fort Lauderdale boat show offers the largest showcase of yachts in the world and attracts yachting enthusiasts from all around the globe. Every boating devotee should visit this show at least once in their lifetime!

We were looking forward to meeting up with Captain Mike as we navigated west toward the Chesapeake Bay. While in the

Atlantic, we trawled at about six to seven knots, trying to catch some fish for lunch, but no luck! So, our alternative was some finger-lickin' fried chicken!

On our way to Norfolk, eating some delicious fried chicken!

About sixty nautical miles later, we encountered the Lucius J. Kellam Jr. Bridge-Tunnel, formerly the Delaware Bay Bridge-Tunnel. This astounding feat of engineering, considered one of the wonders of the modern world, crosses over and under open waters and decreases an automobile's journey south by ninety-five miles. No wonder it is a tourist attraction in and of itself for many motorists. Appreciating the view of this engineering achievement from the ocean really reinforces its magnificence. Construction of additional lanes, which began in 2017, slightly marred this wonder of the modern world.

The bridge-tunnel has a heavy flow of nonstop vessels, both commercial and non-commercial. This day was like all others in the Chesapeake. Many ships and barges were crossing the area, and between them and the ongoing construction, my first mate and I had to have eyes wide open to avoid any catastrophes. It is like cruising the superhighway of the Chesapeake Bay. While one person was on the lookout, the other would watch the navigation and drive the boat.

Traffic on the Chesapeake Bay

After crossing the Chesapeake Bay, we traveled southwest to the Hampton Roads region. One of the world's largest, deepest natural harbors, it sits at the mouth of the Elizabeth, Nansemond, and James rivers. It is also the gateway to Virginia's Historic Triangle. Williamsburg, located five miles inland between the James and York rivers, can be visited through this connection. As America's first planned city, Williamsburg was the center of political activity and saw active debates by George Washington, Thomas Jefferson, and Patrick Henry. Jamestown, located on the James River approximately 2.5 miles southwest of Williamsburg, was the site of the first English settlement in the New World. The third of these important cities in the Historic Triangle, Yorktown, is where the last major battle of the American Revolutionary War took place and English General Cornwallis surrendered his British army to the American Revolution's General George Washington.

After entering the Hampton Roads region, we headed southeast toward the Elizabeth River and our destination of Norfolk, Virginia, a major bustling city of sixty-six square miles with approximately 235,000 people. Norfolk is a four-hundred-year-old port city. The Elizabeth River courses westward, and the Chesapeake Bay stands at the northern border of the Elizabeth River. Eastward, it positions next to Virginia Beach and has the city of Chesapeake to the south. It is a thriving port and home to the world's most extensive naval base, U.S. Naval Station Norfolk. This naval station is home to seventy-five ships, 134 aircraft, fourteen piers, and eleven aircraft hangers. It conducts 275 flights per day and is the hub of navy logistics for the European and Central Command Theater of Operations, which includes the Caribbean. This highly significant naval base is the North American headquarters for the North Atlantic Treaty Organization, NATO. Although it is strictly off-limits, you can see it on a naval base cruise. Aircraft carriers, destroyers, and submarines come to the naval base for repairs and updates.

Additionally, Norfolk is a cultural center, home to Virginia's state opera, stage company, symphony, arts festival, and the MacArthur Memorial. The *Battleship Wisconsin* and the Nauticus Maritime Discover Center, located near each other, offer insight into the naval and maritime experience. Especially interesting for art lovers is the Chrysler Museum of Art, where you will find fifty galleries housing artworks by such famous artists as Pollack, Rothko, and Lichtenstein. It also houses the Atlantic Seaboard's only glassmaking class. If animals are your thing, visit the Virginia Zoo, where you will find tortoises, turtles, lions, lizards, bears, frogs, and other interesting species on their fifty-three-acre park site. At the end of the day you can rest your feet and stop by Benchtop

Brewery for a cold one. This local legend's taste room offers twelve distinct brews on tap, including IPA and pilsner beers with a variety of snacks.

This richness of history, culture, and activities is overflowing, and spending several days here would create a great mini-vacation. Unfortunately, our goal was to get to Fort Lauderdale as soon as possible, so we could only stay in the harbor for the night and could not take in as many sights as we would have liked.

We arrived at our overnight destination, the Waterside Marina in Norfolk, Virginia, at roughly 5 p.m. and met up with Captain Mike. This was a five-star marina! The Waterside only takes overnight reservations, and we were fortunate that we both were able to get into this busy marina. Waterside sits on the Elizabeth River, in the heart of downtown Norfolk, at Intracoastal Waterway mile marker "0." It offers free grocery shuttle service, showers, ice, free Wi-Fi, a floating dock, and power. It can provide accommodations for mega-yachts up to three hundred feet. It is positioned adjacent to the Waterside District dining and entertainment area, which allows for experiencing some of Norfolk's finest dining.

Saturday Night

Waterside Marina Virginia 757-625-3625
Majestic's bow

The marina had an assortment of large, expensive yachts and boats. As we entered Waterside Marina, the current was strong, and the wind was beginning to pick up. I had to dock the boat in reverse, careful not to crash into other boats or the bulky pilings. Right behind us was the *Majestic*, a 201-foot-long mega-yacht, previously owned by Nancy Walton of the Walmart store chain. Its current owners are Bruce Sherman, co-founder of the wealth management company, Private Capital Management; and Derek Jeter, co-owner of the Miami Marlins baseball team. We just stood there speechless for several seconds, totally in awe of this magnificent yacht! This 2007 Feadship yacht can accommodate fourteen guests, along with crew, has a cruising speed of twelve knots, and is equipped with a cinema, hot tub, and gym. All the luxuries of home! The *Majestic* was only one of many magnificent yachts at this marina. After meeting up with Captain Mike and Alex, we decided to stroll around the marina to see these stunning examples of mega-yachts, a show in itself.

Returning to the *Sea Scape*, we all sat down to a dinner of spaghetti and meatballs my first mate, Laurie, prepared. We called it a night early, knowing we all wanted to leave this marina early the following day, when I would cruise along with Captain Mike down the Intracoastal Waterway as we headed to Fort Lauderdale.

OVERVIEW

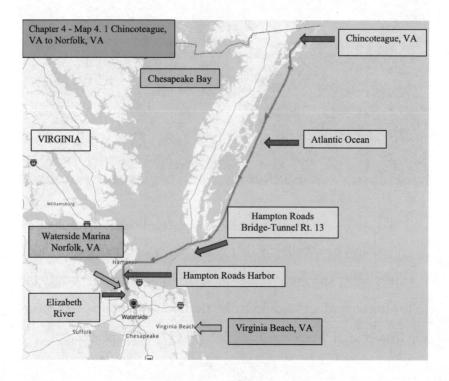

Chapter 4 - Map 4. 1 Chincoteague, VA to Norfolk, VA

Chincoteague, VA

Chesapeake Bay

VIRGINIA

Atlantic Ocean

Hampton Roads Bridge-Tunnel Rt. 13

Waterside Marina Norfolk, VA

Hampton Roads Harbor

Elizabeth River

Virginia Beach, VA

Never Again!

"All men make mistakes, but only wise men
learn from their mistakes"

—*Sir Winston Churchill*

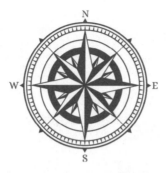

November 7, 2022

Waterside Marina
Norfolk, Virginia
To
Alligator River Marina
Columbia, North Carolina

The weather on the morning of November 7, 2022, was a warm 65 degrees with an expected high of 75, a perfect day for continuing my trip! As planned, we left the Waterside Marina at about 8 a.m. and began following Captain Mike in his thirty-six-foot power catamaran, *The Matrix*. He planned to take the Elizabeth River's southern branch to Deep Creek Lock, then on to Dismal Swamp Canal, connecting to Elizabeth City, from where we would link with the Pasquotank River, then onto the Albemarle Sound, and finally, south to the Alligator River Marina, where we would dock for the night.

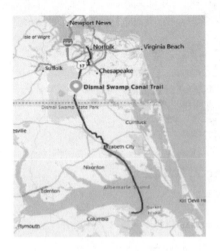 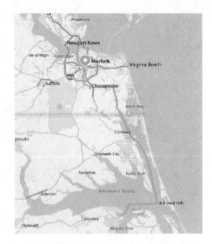

COURSE WE
FOLLOWED

COURSE WE SHOULD
HAVE FOLLOWED

I had never traveled these waters before and did not know what to expect, but I thought Captain Mike was knowledgeable enough to know the best course to follow. Nautical navigation has many complexities and hazards. Knowledge of the shallow zones, underwater obstructions, piers, pilings, treacherous waters, and commercial fishing apparatuses is essential. This trip was an adventure, and little did I know this leg of the trip would not be a very pleasant part of that adventure!

Norfolk's most frequently used course would be to take the southern branch, the Albemarle-Chesapeake Canal, the North Landing River, the Currituck Sound, and finally, the Albemarle Sound. Unfortunately for the *Sea Scape*, Captain Mike chose an alternate route through the Dismal Swamp Canal and then onward until we reached that night's marina.

The 14.5-mile southern branch of the Elizabeth River is one of the busiest commercial ports in the world. It is an urban river that has housed many industries and caused massive ecological concerns. Dry docks, shipyards, processing plants, and a wood treatment facility all called it home.

The wood treatment facility, at one time, dumped an enormous amount of creosote, a substance used to preserve wood, into the waterway. It holds a high probability of carcinogenic properties and was contained in the river's sediment at Money Point, ultimately pooling on the river floor and causing a thirty-five-acre river-floor dead zone of lifelessness. What a horrible assault on nature!

Our ignorance of the consequences of dumping this cancerous substance into a river does not forgive our destruction of a natural water source, one of our most precious natural commodities. Mummichogs, known as Mud Minnows, are small fish that only travel fifty yards during their lifetime. These fish showed a 38 percent concentration of cancerous lesions due to the pollution from the creosote.

The Elizabeth River Project is still working today to clean this river. It has restored the wetlands by removing thousands of tons of contaminated sediment and building a 940,000-seed oyster reef. They are also responsible for constructing Waterfront Park at Paradise Creek in Portsmouth, Virginia, a forty-acre restored salt marsh. It is a wonderland where a naturalist can find a wide assortment of birds, butterflies, box turtles, and foxes to observe, photograph, and relish.

As we traveled southward on the Elizabeth River, we saw buildings, bridges, and abandoned warehouses that appeared weather-beaten, which made the trip remarkable. Interestingly, the naval shipyard lies on the western side of the Elizabeth River in Portsmouth, while the eastern side houses the City of Chesapeake. When traveling south on the Elizabeth River, what grabs one's attention is the many naval ships docked on the east side of the river, while the actual Norfolk Naval Shipyard is located on the western side.

Established in 1767, the Norfolk Naval Shipyard was initially named the Gosport Shipyard after Gosport, England. It acted as a private shipyard facility to repair merchant and British naval ships. In 1929, it was renamed the Norfolk Naval Yard, and in 1945, it acquired the present name of Norfolk Naval Shipyard.

Although the name says Norfolk, it actually resides in the city of Portsmouth and should not be confused with the Norfolk naval base, officially known as Naval Station Norfolk, on Hampton Roads just at the northeast side of the mouth of the Elizabeth River.

The U.S. Navy has four shipyards: two in the eastern United States, one at Portsmouth, Maine, and the other at the Norfolk Naval Shipyard. The third, on the west coast at Puget Sound, is in the state of Washington, and the fourth is at Pearl Harbor, Hawaii. Norfolk Naval Shipyard is the U.S. Navy's oldest, largest, and most comprehensive shipyard. During World War II, the U.S. Navy employed forty-three thousand people at this shipyard and repaired 6,850 vessels there. Today, it rebuilds, restores, and modernizes all types of U.S. naval vessels, from boats to the most advanced nuclear aircraft carriers and submarines. As we passed by, the myriad of ships and vessels harbored at its docks left us awestruck. Each naval vessel was more magnificent than the last. I really would have liked to tour those vessels, but alas, I knew I was too old to join the U.S. Navy and smart enough to know to stay far enough away that I would not get into trouble with them!

Continuing the trip down the southern branch of the Elizabeth River brought us under various bridges. The Norfolk and Portsmouth Belt Line Railroad Bridge; the South Norfolk Jordan Bridge, connecting Chesapeake City to Portsmouth; and the Gilmerton Bridge at South Military Highway just before heading west to Deep Creek and then on to Dismal Swamp Canal.

THE ELIZABETH RIVER SOUTHERN BRANCH

**Norfolk and Portsmouth
Belt Line Railroad Bridge**

**South Norfolk Jordan
Bridge**

Unfortunately, we missed a small, seemingly inconsequential sign pointing to Deep Creek. This sign posted the times for the lock opening connecting Deep Creek to the Dismal Swamp Canal. Although they say that vessels are allowed to moor overnight in the canal by tying up to dolphin pilings, no pilings looked sturdy enough to us for that, so we thought it best to pay attention to the schedule and get through the bridge and lock before nightfall. Nonetheless, we overshot the entrance into the Deep Creek and had to double back.

Deep Creek is a twenty-five-acre, unincorporated area of the City of Chesapeake. Originally a small settlement at the edge of the Great Dismal Swamp Canal, it served as a commercial center during the antebellum period, with a stagecoach stop and a shipping port for the Great Dismal Swamp lumber operations. When Virginia left the Union during the Civil War, the Confederates used Deep Creek to smuggle supplies to the Army. Approximately thirty miles long, it includes the Deep Creek Lock Park. The U.S. Army Corps of Engineers designed the lock to separate the saltwater of Deep Creek from the freshwater of the Dismal Swamp Canal.

DISMAL SWAMP LOCK

Lockmaster's Home

| **The Lockmaster Observing Us Pass** | **Entering the Dismal Swamp Canal from the Deep Creek** |

Our journey to the Atlantic Intracoastal Waterway was only the first of many waterways to be navigated with care, concern, and sometimes laughter. When we reached the lock, we soon found out that the lock operator was the same man who operated the draw

bridge, which was only a quarter of a mile past the lock. He would operate the lock, jump in his car, drive the quarter-mile to the bridge, and then operate the bridge. Then, go back to do it all over again! We almost started to laugh! Amazing! The lock and the bridge were operated according to a corresponding schedule, seven days a week, with the operation of the lock occurring at 8:30 a.m., 11 a.m., 1:30 p.m., and 3:30 p.m., and the draw bridge opening minutes later. The lock could raise a boat approximately eight feet before allowing it entrance into the Dismal Swamp Canal. The canal cuts through the Great Dismal Swamp National Wildlife Refuge. We went through the lock and continued to follow *The Matrix*, Captain Mike's boat.

Captain Mike and I kept in touch by cell phone and VHF radio. He was about a quarter-mile ahead of me. We needed to catch up to Captain Mike to take advantage of the lock and bridge opening he passed through, but he convinced the lockmaster to return and allow us passage so we could proceed together. The bridge is an auto-traffic transport, and each opening delays the driver's ride. So we were lucky and thankful that the lockmaster accommodated us.

Off we went, cruising the twenty-two miles down the Dismal Swamp Canal from Virginia to North Carolina. The U.S. Army Corps of Engineers manages the canal, and the National Register of Historic Places, the Virginia Landmark Register, the National Civil Engineering Landmarks Register, and the National Underground Railroad all list it as an important national landmark. Colonel William Byrd II originally proposed the canal, and it began construction in 1792, taking twelve years to complete. Constructed two centuries ago by enslaved people who worked from both ends, the canal went southward from Norfolk and Chesapeake and northward from the Pasquotank River and Albemarle Sound to meet in the middle of the swamp. This canal and its adjacent areas also acted as a refuge for thousands of escaped enslaved people from the 1680s to the Civil War era.

The notable poet Robert Frost, who read at John F. Kennedy's inauguration, was also connected to this canal. After being shunned by his sweetheart, Elinor White, he traveled from Massachusetts to the Dismal Swamp Canal, hoping to end his life. He crossed into the swamp via the canal route but soon realized that if he died in this wilderness, his love would never know. He then met up with a group of duck hunters, boarded a steamer, and continued his life. Besides being the oldest operating waterway in the United States, the Dismal Swamp Canal holds a great place in American history.

The waters of Dismal Swamp Canal were not the vivid blue of the ocean but rather a brownish gray. Upon initiating our trip on the Dismal Creek Canal, we noticed that as the engines agitated the water, the stir had a noticeable deeper brown, amber, tea-like color caused by the tannins from the trees.

Traveling down the canal, one of the first things you notice is the magnificent foliage of the trees on both sides. Bald Cypress trees form two parallel lines meeting in the distance, with each side reflecting in the water below. These deciduous conifers presented their first dappled signs of red, yellow, and orange as their entry into fall. Their wide supporting bases anchored in the water defied logic. Even the green slime on the water seemed to control our thoughts as it swirled in circles.

For a quick, and I mean quick, moment, you feel as if you've stepped into an artist's painting. It can completely mesmerize if you let it. As we moved along the Dismal Swamp Canal, I noticed the water was not clear, and the green sludge was a warning that here lay trouble.

Captain Mike's boat had a two-and-a-half-foot draft; by comparison, the *Sea Scape*'s draft totals almost five feet. All this, plus accounting for the shaft and propellers, made for treacherous travel down the Dismal Swamp Canal for the *Sea Scape*, especially since the canal's depth never registered greater than five feet and was more likely three and a half feet on average!

Just glancing at the water, I knew that we could have a problem! Debris floated in every direction I looked. Especially present was a green, slimy type of vegetation. In certain regions, duckweed, a small, long, flat, disc-shaped plant less than one-sixteenth inches long, floats just beneath the surface of slow-moving bodies of water and wetlands. Yep! We were in a perfect breeding ground for duckweed! The canal was closed in November 2011 due to abundant duckweed after Hurricane Matthew. I cannot imagine how much duckweed proliferated after that hurricane. Aquatic weeds of lily pads and Virginia creeper vines, logs, branches, and trees, also floating in different spots as we made our journey, made the water treacherous as well. We focused on what floated along the surface, but the debris that had sunk to the bottom of the canal, invisible to our naked eyes, was the most dangerous. The dead logs and vines with their roots anchored in the water were waiting to reach out like giant octopus tentacles and strangle my poor *Sea Scape*. I soon realized there must have been a better route for us, and my body went on alert, tensing at every noise, sound, floating twig, and variance in the water's color. As I soon learned, it was the tiny, flat, oval clusters of duckweed that would ultimately wreak havoc on my engines' strainers.

My boat, being a catamaran, is considered to be multi-hulled, giving it ample stability. I could feel the debris hitting both hulls of  the *Sea Scape*, significantly raising my blood pressure, but at that point, there was no way to turn back. My mind kept reminding me that trouble could lie ahead, and I grew very tense and uneasy. Suddenly, the engines' alarms shrieked! I felt the tension in my gut, and my teeth clenched. What to do? Where could I dock to check the engines? Luckily, we were only about a hundred yards from the Dismal Swamp Canal Welcome Center, which had a small, free dock.

With the dreadful amount of debris floating in the water, the alarm's warning told me the first thing I needed to do was check each engine's strainers. Immediately, I headed to the starboard side's seacock, where a cap topped off the seacock and strainer. Each seacock's housing provides a lever designed to stop water from entering the engine when you remove the strainer from the housing.

Before removing the cap, I had to turn the seacock's lever perpendicular to prevent water from inflowing into the engine compartment. In seconds, I shifted the lever to the perpendicular position, then swiftly removed the cap, which exposed the strainer.

Hurriedly gripping the strainer's small handle, I pulled it straight up and out of the housing. I then transferred the strainer to my first mate who purged all the leaves, debris, and duckweed out of this strainer.

The amount of duckweed was unbelievable, but after a quick cleaning, I was able to wipe the sweat off my brow and take a deep, relieved breath. Ahh! All was good!

Next, we moved on to the port side engine's strainer. This side presented a challenge. I turned the lever and removed the cap, but the water continued to flow into the engine. The lever was not working up to par! I removed the strainer, recapped the housing, and turned the lever back as fast as I could. Again, my first mate cleaned the heavy load of debris from the portside strainer. In a race against time, I turned the lever again, removed the cap, reseated the strainer as quickly as my hands could work, and then closed it. Whew! We did it! It was an exhausting few minutes, but we were ready to roll again. I knew I would have to repeat the process during our journey but wanted to try to wait until we were out of the canal. Off we went, trying to catch up to Captain Mike who had slowed down considerably.

In the meantime, I closely watched how my boat performed. All along the canal, I could feel the debris scraping the hull. I knew the shaft and propellers were being affected, but how much damage they were taking was impossible to gauge at that point. I could drive it, though I felt a significant vibration as we motored along.

I was so distressed by the probable harm the debris was doing to the *Sea Scape* that I did not even enjoy the wonders of the Dismal Swamp Canal. I wanted to take in the beauty around me—the white and bald cypress trees, with their magnificent, tapered-bottom trunks resting in the water and beautiful fall colors of orange and gold, reminiscent of the sweep of an artist's brush; the Great Egrets resting on one leg; and the bald eagles flying overhead.

Still, I was paralyzed and just kept my eyes on the gauges and the water. We traveled along at a snail's pace of about four knots, and with each patch of floating green, I dreaded what might be happening to my strainers and engines. Since it was just after Halloween, we were glad to see

someone had a sense of humor in the swamp. The mannequin pictured is just about how we were beginning to feel. It had been a long, exhausting day filled with unexpected problems. Dismal Swamp Canal was a true adventure, albeit not a positive one. We still had a way to go to get through Elizabeth City, then on to the Pasquotank River, the Albemarle Sound, and the Alligator River Marina that sat at the mouth of the Alligator River. So we chugged along, our eyes ever-watchful, anticipating any problems fermenting in this murky water. At last, we reached the point where we saw a marker announcing our arrival in North Carolina! Finally!

We reached the end of the canal and went through the final lock, South Mills Lock. Goodbye, dismal, Dismal Swamp Canal!

Once through the South Mills Lock, we were at Elizabeth City, North Carolina, a bustling port town whose motto is "Harbor of Hospitality." Elizabeth City prides itself in welcoming transient boaters. It offers forty-eight-hour free boat dockage and engages "Rose Buddies," waterfront ambassadors who greet boaters with a rose, wine, and cheese! What an impressive way to welcome people to your city! This marvelous little town has a historic district near the free docks where you can find retail shops and restaurants. It also houses the Museum of the Albemarle, which boasts many engaging permanent and traveling exhibits. Even Wilber and Orville Wright stopped by this port for provisions.

We quickly stopped at one of the free docks in Elizabeth City to empty our strainers again. Our stay there was so short that we never got to meet the Rose Buddies! Again, duckweed and debris filled the strainers but thankfully, not so much that they set off the alarms. Elizabeth City is another bucket list place of mine to explore!

Leaving Elizabeth City took us under the drawbridge and allowed us to enter the Pasquotank River, one of seven rivers that flow into the Albemarle Sound. Twilight was shortly approaching; the sun would soon be in bed, and I had similar thoughts. It had been a long, stressful day, and my first mate and I were beyond tired. After speaking with Captain Mike, we decided that after chugging along all day, once we reached the wide-open spaces of the Albemarle Sound, it would be time to ramp up our speed and get to Alligator River Marina before it got too dark. I brought the *Sea Scape* up to fifteen knots as we entered the Albemarle Sound, leading us to the Alligator River Marina.

Although my boat had a slight vibration at that point, it was still seaworthy. I could only imagine the damage wrought during our time in the Dismal Swamp Canal but tried to put such worries out of my head so I could pay attention to the course we were on.

When we finally reached Fort Lauderdale and had the entire boat checked out, the mechanic determined that replacing the seacocks would cost $8,000. The damage to the shaft and propellers, most likely from hitting the debris in the Dismal Swamp Canal, wound up costing $34,000 to rectify. My total repairs equaled $42,000! No more Dismal Swamp Canal ever again, and if I never see duckweed again, it will be too soon!

The sun had set, and we were in the Albemarle Sound in the dark. I must admit, traveling in unknown waters at night made me a little nervous, especially when a tanker came very close! My first mate and I kept our eyes open and focused on Captain Mike, who was just ahead of us. This stretch became another harrowing experience on this leg of our journey!

As we headed southwest, we came to the mouth of the Alligator River. The Alligator River Marina sits just before the Route 64, west of the Lindsay C. Warren Bridge, also known as the Alligator River Bridge. With thirty-two slips, a general store, and various other amenities, it is the only fuel stop after the Dismal Swamp Canal, Elizabeth City, and the Pungo River. We absolutely intended to fuel up, knowing that this would be our last chance for a while. We had contacted the marina earlier, and they had two slips waiting for us.

We had been traveling in the dark for quite some time now, and it was getting extremely late. The night was pitch-black, and there was no moonlight to help guide us. We saw the bridge's lights and knew that we needed to make a hard turn to starboard when we came near. The Alligator River Marina sat in the basin alongside the bridge.

The waters outside the channel were shallow; in order not to ground the boat, I needed to stay within the channel markers. So, I relied on three things: my GPS, my first mate, and my spotlight. Hoping the GPS markings were accurate, I used it to guide us through the channel. My first mate lent me her eyes and used her keen sense of vision to check for the channel markers. The *Sea*

Scape's pilothouse roof's movable spotlight, controlled by a lever located on the helm of the pilothouse's dashboard, helped us see what was in front of us.

This event was stressful enough

because of the dark and the unknown waters, but we were also concerned that Captain Mike, who was ahead of us, was driving his boat too fast, at a clip of about fourteen knots in the pitch dark. When driving at night in an unknown area, it feels like you are going at least twice your speed! The darkness, the unknown waters, and Captain Mike's speed made it somewhat scary.

When we pulled into the marina and docked the boat, I realized how stressful that day's part of the journey had been. Between traveling on the Dismal Swamp Canal and driving one hour in the dark to find the marina, my first mate and I were worn out but thankful we had reached our destination safely.

When we reached the Alligator Marina, we were relieved and suddenly starving! What a day! We nourished ourselves with some quick food items we had onboard. We had been keeping a close eye on the weather forecast, and although we were at the tail end of hurricane season, the likelihood of a hurricane was low but still possible. We heard some rattling about a low-pressure system becoming a potential subtropical cyclone forming near the Greater Antilles, just south of Cuba, east of Jamaica, and west of Haiti. I was happy we had completed another leg of our journey but concerned about this weather event. We checked its progress but nothing had changed yet. With that in mind, I knew it was wise to plan for the worst and hope for the best! We all thought it was time to hit the hay, so to speak, and went directly to bed. Just plain exhausted I tried to sleep, but the thought of the possible hurricane lingered. When I last looked at the clock, it read 1 a.m. and sometime after that, I finally fell asleep.

OVERVIEW

Note: BROWN Indicates Route Taken – **Do Not Take this Route** -Never Again!
Red Arrows and Green Line Indicate the **Better Route**

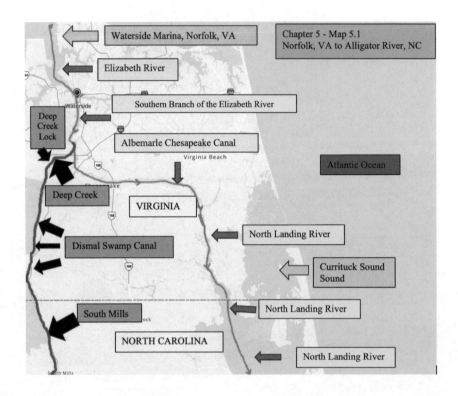

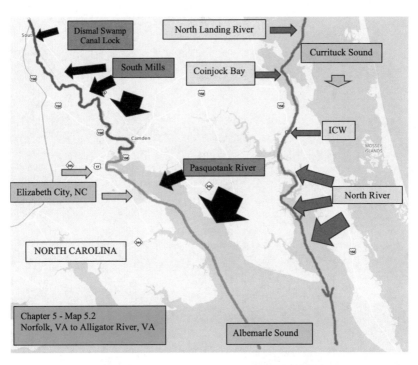

Chapter 5 - Map 5.2
Norfolk, VA to Alligator River, VA

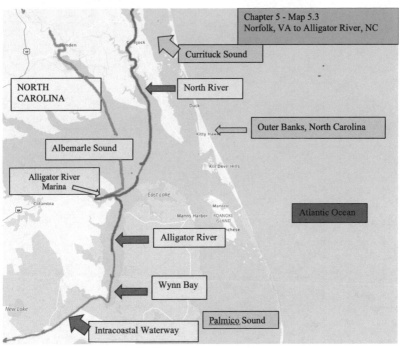

Chapter 5 - Map 5.3
Norfolk, VA to Alligator River, NC

PAINLESS AND PEACEFUL

"Peace is always beautiful!"

–*Walt Whitman*

Early morning
Alligator River Marina, North Carolina

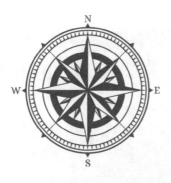

November 8, 2022

Alligator River Marina
Columbia, North Carolina
To
Portside Marina,
Morehead, North Carolina

After a night of rest, the quiet, early morning hours of Tuesday, November 8th, found us refreshed and enjoying the great view of the Lindsay C. Warren Bridge in Columbia, North Carolina. That morning we felt confident that we could overcome any of the new day's challenges—as long as none proved as daunting as last night's drive in the dark or the anxiety we felt going through the Dismal Swamp Canal!

My first mate and I did some general housekeeping chores, wiping down surfaces, emptying trash, pumping out waste, cleaning the toilets, and checking our food supply. When we'd arrived the night before, we docked at the fuel station, but this morning, we

 had to wait for the marina's crew to open it so they could fill us up. Everything on the boat looked up to standard, so we walked over to the marina's small store.

There, we caught up with Captain Mike. Mike and I met over coffee and discussed our plan for the day's voyage. We noted the considerable cloud coverage, indicating that the disturbance, newly named Tropical Storm Nicole, was beginning to cause a significant weather event. That morning, after gaining strength over the warm waters, it had evolved into a tropical storm. Something to watch! The marine weather forecast for the Atlantic Ocean in North Carolina had put out a small craft advisory and predicted winds of twenty to twenty-five knots, with the sea seeing six-to-eight-foot swells. Captain Mike's concern about the wind and weather conditions we would encounter in the Atlantic Ocean raised some red flags. He cautioned us about the potential consequences of the situation, warning us of how fast things could change and of the need to be able to seek shelter and batten down the hatches! His advice was to abandon our original plan of taking the Albemarle Sound to the Pamlico Sound, which ran west of the Outer Banks in North Carolina. Our fear of winding up in the middle of a hurricane outweighed our need to get to our destination on any predetermined schedule. My anxiety began to rise, and as I thought about the hurricane testing our navigational abilities, I wondered how bad it might eventually get. Alarm bells were ringing in my head, and an uneasy feeling settled over me.

We all talked it through and considered all the factors. After using multiple navigation tools, paper charts, piloting books, and electronic equipment, we decided to follow the Intracoastal Waterway (ICW) at the Alligator River. This would include traveling on the Alligator River-Pungo River Canal, then on to the Pungo River and the Pamlico Sound, looping west away from the Outer Banks and onto the Neuse River. From the Neuse River, we would head southeast to Adams Creek, which turns into the Core Creek, all part of the ICW, then the Newport River, and finally, to our destination of the day, Morehead City, North Carolina. It was a longer route and more roundabout way but much safer, with places to shelter should the impending threat of a possible hurricane become a reality.

The Alligator River has an important story attached to it, which we used to divert our minds. "The Alligator River Story," written by an unknown author, has been used at various levels of education to teach, clarify values, support opinions, discuss moral and ethical dilemmas, and even for the sake of debates. The story goes like this:

The Alligator River Story

Once upon a time, there was a woman named Abigail who was in love with a man named Gregory. Gregory lived on the shore of a river. Abigail lived on the opposite shore of the river. The river which separated the two lovers was teeming with man-eating alligators. Abigail wanted to cross the river to be with Gregory. Unfortunately, the bridge had been washed out. So she went to ask Sinbad, a riverboat captain, to take her across. He said he would be glad to if she would consent to go to bed with him preceding the voyage. She promptly refused and went to a friend named Ivan to explain her plight. Ivan did not want to be involved at all in the situation. Abigail felt her only alternative was to accept Sinbad's terms. Sinbad fulfilled his promise to Abigail and delivered her into the arms of Gregory. When she told Gregory about her amorous escapade in order to cross the river, Gregory cast her aside with disdain. Heartsick and dejected, Abigail turned to Slug with her tale of woe. Slug, feeling compassion for Abigail, sought out Gregory and beat him brutally. Abigail was overjoyed at the sight of Gregory getting his due. As the sun sets on the horizon, we hear Abigail laughing at Gregory.

See how you would answer these questions:

1. Why did the characters do what they did?

2. How do their actions demonstrate their values?

3. Who would you like to be like? Who would you not want to be? Why?

4. What values did the characters that disagreed with you? Why?

It proved to be an interesting exercise to absorb our anxiety as we traveled down the ICW. I would have included our answers, but then you might not take the time to formulate your own!

The staff at the Alligator Marina arrived shortly after 7 a.m. Some went to the fuel dock; others to the little house that accommodated people's immediate needs for sundries, small souvenirs, and food items. I told the fuel hands to top off the *Sea Scape*'s tanks. We walked to the little house, where the most mouthwatering smell enveloped our nostrils! A little old lady stood behind the counter, cooking her secret fried chicken recipe! The smell of that chicken was so alluring, it made our tastebuds wake up and shout, "Feed me, now!"

We sat outside and enjoyed a breakfast of fried chicken— which was scrumptious!—and the early morning view of the nearby Lindsay C. Warren Bridge. We had to wait a while for the bridge to open, but we did not object; yesterday's taxing journey, the chicken, and that time to relax seemed like a small reward. Our next segment of this journey involved traveling down the Alligator River and the IWC, hopefully without any major problems!

The Lindsay C. Warren Bridge, also known as the Alligator River Bridge, is a two-lane, 263-foot swing-span bridge, built in 1962. It allows marine traffic entrance into the Alligator River and IWC from the Albemarle Sound. Approximately four thousand vessels pass through this bridge's opening a year. The bridge opens about fifteen times a day, with the entire rotation taking approximately five minutes to open and five minutes to close, plus the added time for boats to pass through. It is a major vehicular thoroughfare leading to the Outer Banks, without which, an additional ninety miles would need to be added to the driver's journey. Whenever the bridge must open for marine traffic, vehicular traffic must stop, and significant delays are caused, especially in the heavily traveled summer season. The bridge gets stuck once or twice during the year and can add a full hour to a vehicle's drive time. Not a convenient way to travel! The bridge is currently due for renovation to begin no later than 2025. The state is building a new bridge just north of the old one that will have a sixty-five-foot, vertical navigable channel clearance, allowing for unimpeded marine and vehicular traffic passage. Still, that day, we had to wait about forty minutes for the old swing-span bridge to open, so we rested outside the marina until it was almost opening time.

263-foot
swing span

With our tanks filled and after our unconventional fried chicken breakfast, our November journey saw the Lindsay B. Warren Bridge opening, and we passed through without any holdup! Many "snowbirds," those northers who travel south for the warm weather when the north is cold and snowy, would take their boats down to Florida using the Alligator River in the early fall. Since we were in late fall and past the "snowbird" migration, we did not see many boats traveling south, but there were still a few. The water of the Alligator River was flat and glass-like on that sunny day, and like a mirror, it reflected the few clouds above. This river was vastly different from the Dismal Swamp Canal. When you

first enter the Alligator River, the central portion of the Alligator River Wildlife Refuge sits to the east. This 152,000-acre wildlife refuge was designated in 1984 to protect pocosins, a type of wetland habitat. Those rare wetlands grow thick layers of peat and shrubby stunted vegetation called shrub bogs. Pond pines, whose crooked growth reaches seventy feet, and Atlantic white cypress, which are eighty to ninety feet tall, dominate this area. This refuge is the habitat for black bears, river otters, ducks, geese, swans, woodpeckers, and some alligators, but its pride inhabitant is the red fox. As you travel down the Alligator River, you may see an occasional bear bathing in the water or a red fox taking a run. We did see a red fox but no bears!

The Alligator River had a broad, expansive width of just over seventeen miles at its mouth at the Albemarle Sound. It remained wide until we had to make a starboard turn to continue toward the Alligator River-Pungo River Canal, which is the ICW. At the turn, it narrows to about 4.5 miles wide, then tapers to a little more than one mile wide before connecting on the ICW. The depth ranges from seven to twelve feet, so my boat was safer, and I felt calmer here than I had felt after the near catastrophe we had in the Dismal Swamp! This leg of our journey was more manageable, though that is not to say that we did not keep vigilant, keeping an eye out for debris and obstructions that could damage the *Sea Scape*.

One of the attendants at the fuel station told us that if you were lucky and observant, you might see an occasional bear swim across the channel, but still, no bears to be seen.

We also missed seeing alligators or deer, but the scenery was beautiful. A line of russet and golden-amber leaves colored the trees

bordering these serene canal waters. The ICW is a pretty straight run at this point, so my first mate and I took advantage of this and each spent time on the stationary bike we have on the *Sea Scape*. Long trips on a boat provide little exercise. We were standing or sitting, and after a while, that got boring, uncomfortable, and confining on the muscles. Our stationary bike offered the exercise, and with my iPad along, I could entertain myself with a movie as I cycled for miles! We also saw some other boats as we went along.

We encountered two bridges while traveling down the Alligator River-Pungo River Canal. The first, the Fairfield Bridge at NC Route 94, a fixed bridge with a sixty-five-foot clearance, appeared at approximately 7.5 nautical miles down the canal. The second, the

Wilkerson Bridge, at US 264, was a fixed bridge with a five-foot clearance that appeared approximately eighteen nautical miles down the canal. Each

bridge was easy to navigate and crowded with other boaters. After the Wilkerson Bridge, we were only about seven-tenths of a nautical mile from the Pungo River, the next phase of the day's journey. We came out of the IWC and entered the Pungo River, sixteen nautical miles from the Pamlico Sound. Along with many trails for kayakers, you can also find plenty of fishing spots on this river whose waters offer various fish, including speckled trout, redfish, and striped bass.

Loblolly pine could be seen all over the banks of the Pungo River. We traveled southwest for approximately seven nautical miles from the Alligator River-Pungo River Canal's point of entry onto the Pungo River. The area we cruised on, the Pungo River, had many fishing boats and some docked sailboats. This journey across the Pungo River  takes about an hour. Afterward, you hook southward and then travel nine nautical miles south toward the Pamlico Sound.

When you reach the Pamlico Sound, you enter the most prominent sound on the Eastern Coast of the United States. The Pamlico Sound is part of an extensive interconnected network of lagoon estuaries formed by the Albemarle Sound, the Currituck Sound, the Croatan Sound, and the Pamlico Sound. The Pamlico

Sound is eighty miles long and fifteen to twenty feet wide, giving you three thousand square feet of open water. The Outer Banks, a collection of barrier islands to the east, separates the Pamlico Sound from the Atlantic Ocean.

The Outer Banks side of the Pamlico Sound is a major playground for watersport lovers. With an average depth of six to eight feet, it is the perfect setup for windsurfing, kiteboarding, kayaking, and paddle boarding—just a few of the types of watersport pursuits you can see people enjoying near this area. Clam grounds and oyster beds are easily accessible there, and the natural wonders are all at their best. Great blue herons, white ibises, snowy egrets, rare white pelicans, and the American bald eagle call Pamlico home.

Another phenomenon is the sunset. We all know that the sun sets in the west, but on Pamlico Sound, you can not only watch the sunrise but also see a stunning sunset due to the utterly unobstructed waterfront view, where no mainland is visible. A rare sight indeed, but one we did not catch because we wanted to make Morehead, North Carolina before dark.

That straight run takes another hour. We came out of the Pungo River into the Pamlico River for a short distance, as it is Pamlico River's entrance to the Pamlico Sound. The Pamlico River is home to several commercial and recreational boats. At this western side of the Pamlico Sound, we needed to stay west to continue in that direction of the Neuse River. With that in mind and knowing that Pamlico Sound is not very deep, we dutifully followed the marked and charted channels as we headed to the Neuse River. The wind, as always, picked up on the open waters of the sound, but the swell of the waves was mild as we continued on our way. Fall is a good time for watersport lovers on the Pamlico Sound. I took out my binoculars and, in the distance, could see kiteboarders and windsurfers. In the air, I noted a parasailer enjoying the breezy ride. As we moved down the sound I could see some snowy egrets, great blue herons, and white pelicans near the shoreline's thickets. A truly enjoyable slice of man and nature enjoying their surroundings. I knew we were making great time and was pleased we would arrive at Morehead City before dark.

We curved westward on the Pamlico Sound toward the Neuse River; traveling at approximately eleven knots, we entered the Neuse about two hours later. Roughly twelve miles down the Neuse, we headed south on Adams Creek, which took us southeast before it turned southwest, around a curve, and then back to the southeast. It was fascinating to see quite a few partially submerged boats on that creek, now old wrecks left untended and half-submerged from past hurricanes.

Traveling south, we reached the Route 101 Bridge, a fixed bridge with a sixty-five-foot clearance. At this point, Adams Creek changes to Core Creek, which is just a continuation of Adams Creek and the ICW.

As the waters of Adams Creek doubled in width, we entered the Newport River. We took the Newport River south, then southeast. From there, the route curves back around southwesterly and heads under the Route 70 Arendell Street Bridge, a fixed-span bridge with a clearance of sixty-five feet. This river leads into Money Island Bay, where you must make a sharp turn west and head around the north side of Sugarloaf Island to where Portside Marina in Morehead City, North Carolina, is located. Morehead City has ten outstanding marinas, including the Morehead City Docks. Unfortunately, the city dock could not accommodate the size of the *Sea Scape*, so we chose the Portside Marina, another exceptional facility.

Named after Governor John Motley Morehead during the

second half of the 1800s, Morehead City is one of two commercial ports in North Carolina known for shipping phosphate. The railroad development made Morehead City North Carolina's first coastal railroad town. The railroad brought many of North Carolina's social and political elite in the summer to Morehead City's posh hotels. The historic district, listed on the National Register of Historic Places, is a railroad town built on high ground away from the shore, between Arendell, Bridges, and Fisher streets, boasting 147 buildings. It has a vast display of architectural styles, including Queen Anne bungalow and craftsman. If not for our goal of reaching Fort Lauderdale within a limited amount of time that would have made for a great little historical side trip.

Happy to enter the marina just as the sun was beginning to set, we took some time to settle ourselves in, relax, drink something cold, and then talk about what we wanted for dinner. Burgers and a salad did us fine. My first mate cooked while I cared for some housekeeping needs. After dinner, we sat on deck listening to the sugary yacht rock music coming off the harbor. It was a relaxing, calm evening, during which we shared a glass of wine and some pleasant conversation, watched the magnificence of a beautiful sunset, and soon went to bed to be ready for tomorrow's part of our voyage. Thankfully the day turned out to be painless and peaceful!

OVERVIEW

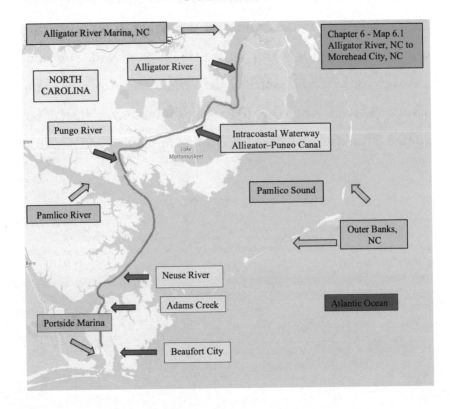

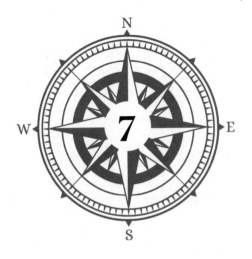

SWEET CAROLINA

"The sea finds out everything you did wrong"

—*Francis Stokes*

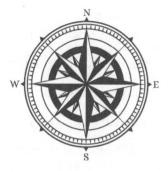

November 9, 2022

Portside Marina
Morehead City, North Carolina
To
Bridge Tender Marina
Wilmington, North Carolina

Today, we rose at about 6 a.m., our average waking time, ready to continue our journey on the Intracoastal Waterway of North Carolina's Crystal Coast. The fall temperature was in the high fifties. The galley's one-cup coffee maker supplied the aroma of coffee, to which we added some Baileys Irish Cream-flavored coffee creamer to perk up the taste. We sat with our coffee and thought about the day ahead. Captain Mike and his first mate, Andrew, joined us that morning, and we discussed our day's plan.

As we sat and sipped the sweet, aromatic Baileys-flavored coffee, we discussed what distance we should undertake for that day. All though Nicole was some five hundred nautical miles away, we were starting to feel the early development of the unstable atmosphere; she was spinning. The weather service predicted it would change to Hurricane Nicole and move northward from Eastern Florida coast over the next day or two. Already feeling the winds blowing hard at about twenty to twenty-five knots, with some gusts reaching over forty, our goal became getting to safety before nightfall. We considered extending our docking accommodations for an additional night. We knew it was hard enough trying to find one-night accommodations for two boats, never mind two consecutive nights. We also realized there might be a problem if many of the boats, typically at sea, decided to come in to find safer shores. Knowing we were not in any immediate danger, we decided to try to reach Bridge Tender Marina in Wilmington, North Carolina. Once we were nearer to that location, we figured we would re-assess the weather conditions and decide whether to go beyond that point.

Before launching, we discussed our plan for departing the marina and decided it would be easier if we backed up the *Sea Scape*, which was moored at the fuel dock, and then moved forward. We would meet Captain Mike and *The Matrix*, our traveling partner, in the bay right outside the marina.

During our stay at the Portside Marina, we heard banging and hissing, all night long. When we arrived the night before, it was late, and dark and we were too exhausted to notice the massive destroyer on our starboard side at the next marina. However, the next morning, we quickly learned that the banging and hissing sounds were coming from that destroyer docked close to the marina. We could see people working on repairs and renovating the ship. The destroyer's position kept it guarded and difficult to approach, which we assumed was to evade radar detection. I knew I would have to be careful and keep a significant distance from her to avoid being boarded by the Coast Guard safeguarding her. Seeing her awesomeness up close, I imagined this breathtaking destroyer on some exotic mission. Out of respect for our mighty U.S. Navy, we forgot about the noises that annoyed us throughout the night.

After untying our lines around 7:30 that morning, with skies partly cloudy and the wind whipping all around us, we tuned into VHF channel 14 for communications and slowly backed up and exited the fuel dock using our camera system and wireless headphones. We held our course a few hundred feet later in the bay, waiting for *The Matrix* to leave its slip and approach us. Captain Mike maneuvered *The Matrix* toward us in his usual skillful and competent manner. Seeing his approach, we gave way and followed *The Matrix* to the Intracoastal, a reasonably short distance from our previous night's dockage at Portside Marina.

Traveling west on the Bogue Sound, we entered the Intracoastal; we heard the howling wind whistling throughout and hoped the day would go well. Even before listening to the weather updates, I knew something was happening. Since the Intracoastal is somewhat shallow, even the smallest waves were cresting in one direction, with spray at their tops. Those surface waves, which flowed easterly by southeasterly, revealed the strength and direction of the wind. It became clear to me that the weather disturbance, named Nicole, moving in from the Caribbean, was already affecting the direction and speed of the wind and waves of the Carolinas' waters. Of course, every hour or two, I checked the VHF weather stations for updates. The weather began to solidify our choice of Wilmington, North Carolina as our next destination.

As we left Morehead City, North Carolina, we entered Bogue Sound, a lagoon separating Bogue Banks, a twenty-one-mile-long barrier island from the North Carolina mainland. It is part of North Carolina's Crystal Coast and the Southern Outer Banks. It begins at Harkers Island, North Carolina, and extends approximately twenty-five miles to this barrier island's western point of Lands End.

A little over a century and a half ago, investors led by John Motley Morehead purchased six hundred acres from Bridges Arendell Sr. A parcel of land, they named Shepherd's Point Land Company in Morehead City, was incorporated in 1858, and was named after then-governor John Motley Morehead, the "Father of Modern North Carolina." This large port city became a major transport center for shipping tobacco, grain, salted meats, fish, and lumber to England. It also supplied the shipping industry with tar, pitch, rosin, and turpentine. One key action of Governor Morehead was to ensure that the railroad system would carry people to its fair shores. Today, the Crystal Coast holds a noteworthy place in North Carolina's tourism industry with its exciting beach communities. It is a beautiful, relaxing place, giving visitors a break from life's everyday hustle and bustle. During the summer months, you will find a substantial number of sun-worshipers at this summer playground, flocking to its wide variety of hotels, rental properties, marinas, cultural events, and restaurants, especially the ones that serve delectable seafood. It proudly hosts the annual North Carolina Seafood Festival, a feast for any seafood lover.

Only two bridges cross the sound, allowing automobile entry into the barrier island. One is at Morehead City, which takes you into Atlantic Beach, and the second is at the opposite end of the island at Cape Carteret, where you gain entry to Bogue Sound at Emerald Isle.

Just about a nautical mile from Portside Marina, on the Morehead City side of the Bogue Sound, the *Sea Scape* and *The Matrix* crossed under the Atlantic Beach Bridge, which connects Morehead City to Bogue Island. Sitting at ICW mile marker 206.7, this bridge has a ninety-foot horizontal clearance. After passing this bridge, we glimpsed the beautiful Bogue Sound. Coastal towns on its southern side include Atlantic Beach, Indian Bay, and Emerald Isle, and you will find Morehead City, Beaufort, and Swansboro on the opposite, northern inland side. Only three miles wide, we got to see both the northern and southern shoreline. Beautiful seaside homes sit at the water's edge, long extended docks stretch out from tree-lined sections of the coast, and small islands all provide summer enjoyment for countless vacationers. If you are a mariner, fisherman, kayaker, watersport enthusiast, or just a sun-worshipper, these shores offer the best of summertime recreation. My first mate and I agreed that it is a great place to visit and live year-round.

As we neared the end of the Crystal Coast, we approached the B. Camron Langston Bridge, named after a North Carolina highway commissioner who worked to develop the bridge but died before its completion. Located at ICW mile marker 226.0, it is more commonly known as the Emerald Island Bridge or the Emerald Drive-Route 58 Bridge. This fixed bridge has a vertical clearance of sixty-five feet and a horizontal clearance of ninety feet. Nearly two nautical miles past this bridge, we came to the end of the Bogue Banks barrier island, where it opens to one of the first of many inlets we have encountered. All these inlets allow a boater to meet with the Atlantic Ocean.

Before using these inlets, smaller vessels should verify their suitability, and as a captain, you must know your boat, what it can and cannot do. Depending on the conditions in the Atlantic Ocean, the waters near the inlets can rapidly shift. Your boat must track well in a following sea—in other words, a sea where the water, waves, and surface correspond to the movement of the tide. It must navigate well at low speeds to allow you to negotiate waves, buoys, jetties, and other objects you may encounter. As captain, you must do your homework. Don't be afraid to ask the locals about the inlet. Study the inlet on your maps, know the tide flow schedule, and watch the direction and power of the waves. You must be able to see and feel how all this affects your vessel. The appropriate skills are needed, along with comprehensive knowledge of your boat, to maneuver an inlet. Keep in mind that by just waiting a short time, a rough inlet can greatly calm down, and most importantly, remember to avoid crossing an inlet in the dark, the most dangerous time to do so. Today's waters were beginning to see the effects of Nicole, who was on her way, with small but distinct waves—a reminder, as always, to remain constantly aware of all marine conditions.

Nearing the island's end, we approached Swansboro, where we needed to head west. As we rounded this coast, we saw a small island upon which resided a single, small house. An interesting sight! After a quick investigation on our iPad, my first mate found that this small island house was for rent. Imagine that! Your own private island to vacation on! It included a small cabin with two queen-sized beds, one upstairs in the loft and one on the main floor, plus an inflatable bed. When needed, a generator provided air-conditioning or heat and hot water for the outdoor shower. Also included in the description were a rain barrel, four kayaks, a fireplace, a grill, and a tent. It was also listed as dog-friendly, so you are welcome to bring Fido along! You can find it on Airbnb under Eco-Glam Swansboro, North Carolina. What a unique experience!

Past this little island, heading northeast, the waterways became somewhat narrower, tighter, and riskier. You needed to keep your eyes open and use all your senses. The waterway grew less navigable, with shallow areas marked in green on the map and many more green and red buoys to guide the way.

Unfortunately, the moment came when I failed to take my own advice; somewhere in that area, while I should have been more attentive to this waterway, I got caught up looking at an anchored sailboat on my port side not too far from our location. Within a split second, I inadvertently took my eyes off my route, and BOOM!

All of a sudden, my boat started jerking. My heart raced, and my adrenaline spiked. I started sweating, conjuring up scenarios of needing to call for help because although I did not want to believe it, my first thought was, *"Did I just run aground?"* Many more types of thoughts went through my mind. I knew that my boat was heavy—forty-four tons to be exact—and that could mean all kinds of structural damage. What could have happened? I feared serious damage to my boat! What a nightmare, but my professional training had taught me to stay calm, think, and assess. I took a deep breath and looked at my instruments. My sounder said that I was in twelve feet of water. So how could I have gone aground? After my assessment, I asked myself, *"Is something stuck in the propeller?"*

I focused and remained calm enough to manage the controls. I threw the shifters into reverse. As the boat retreated, a red buoy came into view. Realizing I ran over a buoy, now caught by the *Sea Scape*, I pulled further back, and the boat freed itself. By some token of luck, the gods were in my favor. I was not grounded! I watched through the pilothouse window as all this played out like a slow-motion movie. I took a deep breath and let go of the fear and utter horror of how horrible this could have been. I began to slow things down inside me and regained my calm. My first mate rushed around and checked everything possible. When she signaled that all was well, I said a silent prayer and gave thanks for being saved and rescued from this earthly nightmare. After another quick check of everything, I knew I had been able to get off the buoy with no damage to my boat. The *Sea Scape* was safe! What a relief! I would surely say my prayers before I went to sleep that night and swore that not for even a second, ever again, would I take my eyes off the waterway ahead of me.

After our short turn west, we navigated the *Sea Scape* slightly south and southwest following the Intracoastal Waterway. Anyone traveling this section of the ICW will notice areas along the shoreline filled with vegetation, grasslands, and trees. Low-lying vegetation can be seen along the port side facing the ocean. Although vegetation grows in the water, it is less dense and closer to the shoreline than on the Alligator River or the Pungo River. One crucial point to realize here is that once out of the Bogue Sound, the Intracoastal becomes relatively narrower, so it is important to pay attention. The ocean is close enough to be seen from the boat, and I easily imagined that in extreme weather conditions, these two separate bodies of water could easily become one. We wanted to avoid being in those waters if a hurricane was coming in at full force.

As we continued down the Intracoastal with a vigilant eye, we passed through Carteret County, with its sandy beaches and dunes. The weather was beginning to change; the clouds started to disappear, replaced by a beautiful, clear sunny day. By midday, the temperatures were reaching well into the seventies in the sun. The next part of the Intracoastal stood in sharp contrast to the beaches and dunes of Carteret County, where no people or homes could be seen. Here, signs of life abounded. We saw many homes lined up along the banks on our starboard side, each with docks and anchored boats. On the port side, we saw no homes, only masses of dunes protecting the natural environment from floods and erosion.

We traveled past the entrance to Queens Creek and further on past the entrances to Bear Creek, Morgan Creek, and Freemans Creek, all of which abut Marine Corps Base Camp Lejeune. This home of "expeditionary forces in readiness" is a 246-square-mile United States military base located on the northern shore of the ICW and occupies fourteen miles of shoreline. Their 170,000 employees account for not only active-duty Marines but also a wide variety of other workers who help keep the base running. Many have heard of the lawsuits initiated because of contaminated well water sources from the base, which affected almost one million people. They were exposed to chemicals used in degreasing and cleaning operations at two dry cleaning businesses located inside the base and chemicals used at an off-base fuel depot. This contamination caused not only a wide variety of cancers but also congenital disabilities and an assortment of other serious health problems. Sometimes, the base will conduct firing exercises and close the ICW down for a few hours for everyone's safety. Today, though, the camp was not conducting any exercises, so we continued past it undeterred.

After approximately nine nautical miles, past Hammocks Beach State Park on the ICW, we entered Hubert County, where we approached the Oslow Swing Bridge at ICW mile marker 204.7. Marine Corps Base Camp Lejeune began constructing a new bridge in October 2022. The current bridge connecting the camp to Oslow Beach is nearly seventy years old and has a high maintenance cost. This construction may cause partial or complete closure of the waterway in the future. Still, we did not encounter any difficulties gaining access to the opening of the swing bridge.

The waters of the Intracoastal, past the Bogue Sound, were rough in many places. We needed to follow the channel markers closely or risk quickly running aground—or hitting a buoy, as I had previously done—by not being vigilant. I watched every marker, wave, and buoy diligently. One bad buoy experience, I decided, was one too many!

Once past the Oslow Bridge, the scenery drastically changed. No homes or docks, as we had seen lining the shore, were apparent. Now only beautiful marshlands and banks, with tall reeds and trees. The sun was glistening off our bow, and though I wanted to linger over the view, my mind told me to keep my eyes on the waterway.

As the *Sea Scape* traveled down the Intracoastal, we glided under the Top Sail Island Bridge, better known as the NC 210 Highway Bridge, at ICW mile marker 252.3. It has a vertical clearance of sixty-five feet with a horizontal clearance of ninety feet. This height appears to be the standard for newer bridges.

But no fishing for us! The Intracoastal along the North Carolina barrier islands provided us a look at several beach towns connected by bridges that we had to cross under. Our journey continued, and approximately seven and a half nautical miles from Top Sail Island Bridge, we encountered another fixed bridge with a sixty-five-foot vertical clearance, the Surf City/Roland Avenue Route 50 Bridge at mile marker 260.7. We cruised under the bridge and down the Intracoastal past Surf City, a typical, good-time family beach town.

Only two more bridges remained to pass through before we reached our marina for that evening's respite. Thirteen and a half miles straight on the Intracoastal, we encountered the seventy-three-year-old Figure Eight Island Swing Bridge. The bridge opens up every half hour on the hour, and we were lucky enough to just catch the bridge opening. The bridge tender was extremely pleasant, waving to us as we passed. Onward we went!

We were only four nautical miles to our destination, the Bridge Tender Marina, just past the Wrightsville Beach Bridge. This bridge connects the City of Wilmington to the town of Wrightsville. Officially known as the C. Heide Trask Memorial Bridge, named after a North Carolina highway commissioner, this 171-foot-long bascule bridge opens every hour on the hour. Our luck was still with us, and we only had to wait five minutes.

We slowed and took our time approaching the bridge. After it opened, we realized that the Bridge Tender Marina was only two-tenths of a nautical mile further down on our starboard side! It welcomes transient boaters with sixty-five slips and a 350-foot floating dock. Accommodating boats up to two hundred feet, with an eighteen-foot docking depth, it offers full services, with free cable

television and high-pressure, wash-down water.

We knew that was far enough for that day's leg of our journey. We had no turns to make and just pulled in. The staff were extremely pleasant and accommodating. It was late afternoon, around four o'clock. The *Sea Scape* and *The Matrix* both got dock space on the bulkhead in the front. We finished all the regular docking duties, and as the sun began to set, enjoyed a celebratory dinner on the aft deck of the *Sea Scape* with Captain Mike and his first mate. The

food was good and the company even better, but our main topic of conversation was the approaching hurricane, Nicole, which forced us to focus on the next day's docking destination of North Myrtle Beach.

Nicole was approaching landfall either that or the following night, though forecasters still could not pinpoint the path of her direct hit. Our job was to keep our eyes and ears tuned to any information regarding her path and expected time of landfall. But eyes had grown heavy after our full day's journey; we needed time to rest. So off to sleep we all went until the next morning, when our journey would resume.

OVERVIEW

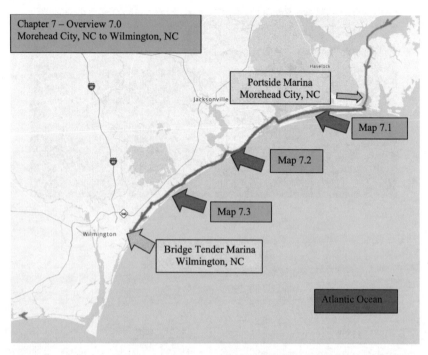

Chapter 7 – Overview 7.0
Morehead City, NC to Wilmington, NC

Portside Marina
Morehead City, NC

Map 7.1

Map 7.2

Map 7.3

Bridge Tender Marina
Wilmington, NC

Atlantic Ocean

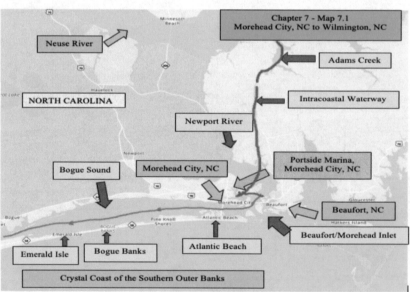

Chapter 7 - Map 7.1
Morehead City, NC to Wilmington, NC

Neuse River

Adams Creek

NORTH CAROLINA

Intracoastal Waterway

Newport River

Portside Marina,
Morehead City, NC

Bogue Sound

Morehead City, NC

Beaufort, NC

Beaufort/Morehead Inlet

Emerald Isle

Bogue Banks

Atlantic Beach

Crystal Coast of the Southern Outer Banks

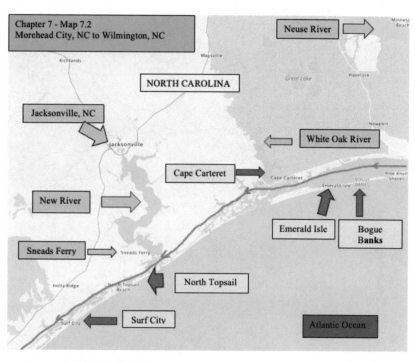

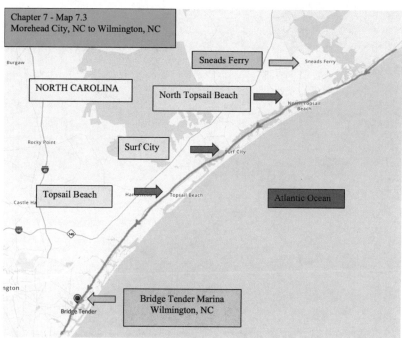

THE BRUNSWICK ISLANDS

"Waves are not measured in feet and inches;
they're measured in increments of fear."

—*Buzzy Trent*

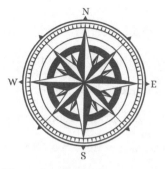

November 10, 2022

Bridge Tender Marina,
Wilmington, North Carolina
To
Harbourgate Marina Club,
North Myrtle Beach, South Carolina

Everybody has a morning routine, and we were no different. By now, our lively little group of four had fallen into a pattern, rising at around 6 a.m. and starting with coffee, the first thing on everyone's mind. We would have a cup with Captain Mike, his first mate, Andrew, and Lauri, and after a light breakfast, while gibberjabbering about anything that came to mind, we would decide to get ready to make way. But today felt different. We knew that Hurricane Nicole would most likely make landfall somewhere near Vero Beach, Florida, that evening, and if it did, it would only be about four hundred miles away, bringing heavy wind and rain.

We only had that day for last-minute preparations for the

unknown chaos we could face. We had enough provisions to last several days, so food was not a problem. We had filled up at the fuel dock. We double-checked to ensure we had enough lines and fenders to double-secure the boat. Depending on Nicole's path, the one thing in question was where we could secure shelter for the boat and ourselves for at least one night and possibly more.

We discussed the distance we would travel that day, which would enable us to safely reach the Myrtle Beach, South Carolina area, approximately sixty nautical miles away. We also sensed that finding refuge that night might be especially challenging as others were traveling down the ICW and would be making similar preparations for the storm. It was November, and when planning our day, we needed to consider the shorter amount of daylight available, with the sun setting around 5 p.m. Had it been spring, the sun would have been with us until 8 p.m. After recently traveling after dark to reach the Alligator River Marina, I did not relish the thought of having to do it again. Our plan took into account the Intracoastal Waterway, with its many no-wake zone speed areas, requiring a maximum of roughly seven to eight knots. With that in mind, our calculations had us arriving at approximately late afternoon or early evening. Our goal was to get to the next port and seek shelter. As we moved southward toward Nicole's path, our intuition warned us about the possible lack of marina docking space to accommodate the *Sea Scape* and *The Matrix* for one night, never mind two. The morning winds were lighter than they had been the previous day. However, we knew things could worsen as we continued south toward the hurricane.

We departed the Bridge Tender Marina from Willington, North Carolina, around 8 a.m. and began our trip down the Intracoastal Waterway. Within half an hour, we approached the Masonboro Inlet leading to the Atlantic Ocean. With Nicole on the way, we did not want to come out through this inlet into the Atlantic, so we continued past the Masonboro Inlet on the ICW.

Masonboro Island, the largest untouched barrier island along North Carolina's southern shores, rested directly to our port side. Those 8.5-mile-long southern shores contain 5,653 acres of natural marsh and tidal flats. If you are into primitive camping, meaning you must bring everything you need in on foot and take everything you have used out with you when you leave, this area is for you. It is accessible only by boat or private ferry for a fee. Sounds like a lot of work to me, but naturalists or those who wish to study nature would be right at home, I guess. This past October 2022, Masonboro Island was the site of a record-breaking number of loggerhead turtle nests. These endangered turtles are now protected by North Carolina law as coastal development eliminated many of their nesting sites. Undeveloped Mansboro Island, therefore, provides the perfect nesting site. After laying their eggs, the turtles only have a one in one thousand chance of seeing their babies hatch, which is usually a sixty-day process, and make their crawl out to sea. As we traveled along Masonboro Island, we kept our eyes open for any loggerheads but did not see even one.

Seven and a half nautical miles down the Masonboro Island coast, we reach the Carolina Beach Inlet and we approached the town of Sea Breeze. The sights in that town were reminiscent of a view on the Jersey shore, with similar beach homes and apartment buildings. At approximately 9:20 a.m., we traveled another 1.3 nautical miles and turned westward into Snow's Cut and then under the Snow's Cut Bridge, a fixed bridge with a sixty-five-foot vertical clearance. By 9:50 a.m., we entered the Cape Fear River. The wind whipped up to thirty knots, with much stronger gusts, and the waters were visibly rougher. But the *Sea Scape*, being a forty-four-ton powered catamaran, cruised through these waters without much sway. We sailed around Cape Fear, made infamous by the movie of the same title.

For anyone who has not seen *Cape Fear*, it is a classic thriller. The main character, a convicted rapist, played by Robert De Niro, just released from prison, has only one goal: to hunt down the public defender, played by Nick Nolte, whom he blames for his imprisonment. He follows the protagonist on the Cape Fear River. Then, well, you should really watch the movie if you haven't already. Those of you who have will surely remember DeNiro's outstanding portrayal for which he won an Oscar. Warning: This film contains violent scenes and some graphic content.

We thought it would be apropos to see it again, so we pulled it up on the iPad to watch the following night! Yikes—DeNiro's portrait of that maniac will scare the pants off you every time you see it!

On our journey down the Cape Fear River, we noted an area known as the Frying Pan Shoals, also known as the Frying Pan Handle, which is a 28-mile-long shifting group of shallow shifting shoals. Due to its many shipwrecks, it is called the "Graveyard of the Atlantic". It sits at a ninety-degree angle to the Cape Fear Inlet when going to sea and is at least seventeen miles from the shore into the ocean. Its importance lies in that if one wants to go north, one must travel out at least twenty miles to avoid this shoal offshore before turning north. The Cape Fear Inlet ends with Bald Head Island on its south side and Southport on the port side.

After traveling down Cape Fear River (the continuation of the inlet) and reaching the mouth of the inlet, one must turn southwest across the Cape Fear Inlet to enter North Carolina's Brunswick Islands, which we did at about 10:30 that morning. The Brunswick Islands are a group of barrier islands between the Outer Banks, North Carolina, and Myrtle Beach, South Carolina. We would pass six towns in this group of barrier islands, each with its own blissful sand and surf shoreline, offering a breezy, carefree, delightful summer retreat to those making it their habitat year-round or just for the summer season.

One of the most distinctive things about living here is that the sun both rises and sets on the ocean in late fall and early spring. Beaches generally face south, but here, they face east and west, and in the late fall and early spring, the sun, if far enough south, gives a glimpse of both a beautiful sunset and the magnificence of sunrise. We were hoping to enjoy this phenomenon, but the incoming clouds from Nicole hampered our view that morning, and we expected the same for the evening's sunset. Tomorrow's weather also predicted rain, ruling out any beautiful sunrises or sunsets that day—maybe next year!

As we turned west, from the mouth of Cape Fear and into the ICW at Southport, we entered Oak Island. If you ever see a bumper sticker with OKI, it's their moniker for Oak Island. Oak Island, a thirteen-mile long, one-mile wide island of the Brunswick Islands barrier chain, encompasses the locations of Fort Caswell, Caswell Beach, and Oak Island.

Fort Caswell was located directly to the southeast of us, and Bald Head Island was to our northeast. Fort Caswell, a mason garrison constructed in the early 1800s, was created to guard the entrance to the Cape Fear River. Today, it serves as the North Carolina Baptist Assembly coastal retreat and conference center, available for members of the Baptist Church and other Christian groups. The Baptist State Convention of North Carolina bought the fort from the federal government in 1949 and developed it into a full convention center. With a boat dock, hotel, boy barracks, dormitories, cottages, a lodge, and its convention center, it can supply all the needs of those who visit with food, linens, modern technology at the convention hall and classrooms, and meeting spaces for a variety of group sizes. It is truly a unique and beautiful place to gather.

Caswell Beach is the next town along the ICW and is the least populated beach town of the Brunswick Islands. Adjacent to Fort Caswell, this beach town has a winter population of approximately four hundred, which increases to roughly two thousand during the summer season. The large homes, tucked behind sand dunes, provide a perfect view of the frothy waves. The Oak Island Lighthouse, built in 1958, stands guard. If you are a lighthouse enthusiast and wish to climb to the top of this landmark, you should make a reservation six months in advance during the crowded summer season.

Continuing along we slid under the sixty-five-foot clearance of the fixed Oak Island Bridge, a short distance from here, at ICW mile marker 311.8. Oak Island is a characteristically North Carolina beach town with a winter population of approximately eight thousand and a summer population of fifty thousand. Wow! That's a lot of people taking in the perfume of the sea and eager to do all the wonderful summertime activities! As we passed by, we saw house after house lining the beach, much like the coastal-lined seaside towns of my home state of New Jersey.

As we neared the end of Oak Island, we crossed under another sixty-five-foot-tall fixed bridge, the Middleton Bridge, located at ICW mile marker 311.8. This route led us to another of the Brunswick Islands, Holden Beach. *National Geographic Traveler* lists this 8.4-nautical-mile, beachy island as one of the best family beaches in North Carolina. Families return to enjoy the family fun atmosphere year after year, enjoying their children while fishing from either the Holden Beach Pier or from a charter boat, or crabbing, biking, or swimming. More adult-friendly activities include golfing on a championship course, shopping for local arts and crafts, watching the shrimp boats come and go, enjoying an afternoon cocktail on a floating tiki bar, or just indulging in one of the many epicurean treats at numerous family-friendly restaurants. All great activities for everyone who visits, but not that day; summer was over, and all the tourists had gone home.

In New Jersey, we call those tourists "Bennies," derived from the nickname given to non-local spectators attending the Benihana Offshore Grand Prix, which was the largest Atlantic Ocean powerboat race in the world held near Point Pleasant Beach, NJ. The nickname stuck and is now used to describe any tourist to the NJ shore. Today, Bennies are usually loud, flashy visitors from another part of the state or those not from New Jersey at all!

As we flowed down the IWC, we saw the many surfside homes

lining the beach, interspersed with the many natural habitats of the island. A few miles into Holden Island, we passed under the Holden Beach Bridge, NC 130, the only road leading into the island. Ocean Isle Beach is the next of the Brunswick Islands on the ICW. Like Holden Island, Ocean Isle has only one bridge leading into it. The Ocean Isle Beach Bridge allows the NC 904 traffic over the ICW and into the island. This tiny, five-mile-long island has Tubbs Inlet to its west and Shallotte Inlet to its east, allowing direct access to its shores. Its natural habitat, a breeding ground for deer, foxes, and sea turtles, sits on the southern part of the Brunswick Islands and has been called the "Gem of the Brunswick Islands."

The last island in the Brunswick Islands chain, Sunset Beach, has been named one of the twenty-one best beaches in the world by National Geographic. This 2.7-nautical-mile island has beaches sitting east to west and allows for viewing the most glorious sunrises and sunsets on the East Coast of the United States. As we come to the end of this island, we pass into South Carolina, placing us approximately eight nautical miles west of our destination, Harbourgate Marina, in North Myrtle Beach, SC.

After we passed Sunset Beach, the ICW veered slightly northwest and became known as the Little River. Here, the Little River Inlet comes in from the ocean and enters the ICW. Continuing our course down the river took us to Harbourgate Marina. Only then did we find two slips for the *Sea Scape* and Captain Mike's *Matrix*. However, with the approaching hurricane that evening, we could not find space to house us both in the same area. Therefore, Captain Mike took *The Matrix* to a marina just north of Harbourgate.

Harbourgate Marina Club, a full-service marina with an additional watersport rental facility, connects to a set of rentable condominiums. The condominium club offers a pool, hot tub, and gym, and the marina accommodates boats in its one hundred wet slips. It was indeed a magnificent marina!

The marina allowed us to tie up at the fuel station dock. Hurricane Nicole was to make landfall early that night in Southern

Florida. Weather reports told us to expect heavy oncoming winds.

We carefully tied our lines off the boat and employed extra fenders to protect it. With our reservation for that night at the fuel dock, we knew we had to leave early in the morning because another vessel was coming in and had reserved the slip for that night.

After securing the boat, we walked up the walkway to the marina office and met an extremely helpful woman named Angela—our angel sent to us from above! Somewhat nervous about not having a two-night stay available at this marina, we explained our and *The Matrix*'s situation and asked Angela for help forming a plan for the following evening. We figured on traveling to Georgetown, South Carolina. My first mate, Lauri, Angela, and I began calling marinas, seeking to reserve a slip for the next day. Finding someone as welcoming, generous, and outgoing as Angela was outstanding. Listening to her, I could tell that people working in marinas had a sense of brotherhood. She was so very willing to take the time and speak on our behalf. The next day, we would plan to travel to Georgetown, South Carolina. With Angela's help, we secured a reservation for the *Sea Scape* and *The Matrix* for the following night at Harborwalk Marina, where we could rest our boats and ourselves. Harbourgate Marina is lucky to have such a magnificent person representing them.

As we left the marina office we noticed a black cat eating her dinner. Most would say having a black cat is begging for bad luck, but I like to believe the opposite. Both she and especially Angela brought us good fortune! Relieved,  we returned to the *Sea Scape* and contacted Captain Mike with our good news.

 We had a small, quiet dinner without Captain Mike and his first mate, Andrew. We missed the conversation and banter that glued us together as a two-boat team. After eating, we called Sarah, Lauri's daughter, who was in Fort Lauderdale.

She told us the hurricane was a short distance from Fort Lauderdale, our final destination. The predicted path for Hurricane Nicole at this point was east, crossing over Florida, and then turning northward, where it would lose some of its strength. Sarah said the rains were coming down heavily, and the wind was howling! The tides were high and had come over our dock at my Fort Lauderdale house. Hurricane Nicole may have landed at Vero Beach, Florida, but its powerful winds and rains had spread ninety miles to Fort Lauderdale. It sounded scary, but we hoped that by the time we got to Fort Lauderdale, Nicole would have moved up northward and dissipated, allowing us to miss the major brunt of that horrific storm.

We were due to arrive in Fort Lauderdale around November 17th, in six days, so the odds of us encountering trouble from the hurricane were slim, but as they say, you can't fool with Mother Nature. She has a mind of her own. So respectfully, we watched and waited as we traveled, hoping all would be clear. With the thought of Nicole on our minds, we cleaned up after dinner and knew it was time to settle into bed for a good night's sleep. We wanted to be ready to meet up with Captain Mike and *The Matrix* the following day and resume our journey!

OVERVIEW

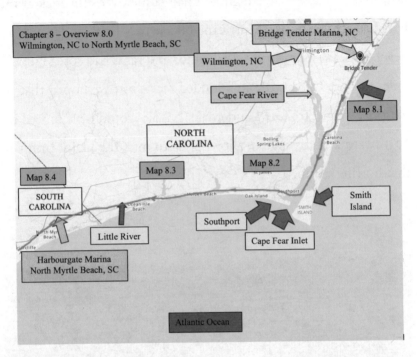

Chapter 8 – Overview 8.0
Wilmington, NC to North Myrtle Beach, SC

Bridge Tender Marina, NC

Wilmington, NC

Cape Fear River

Map 8.1

NORTH
CAROLINA

Map 8.2

Map 8.3

Map 8.4

SOUTH
CAROLINA

Smith
Island

Little River

Southport

Cape Fear Inlet

Harbourgate Marina
North Myrtle Beach, SC

Atlantic Ocean

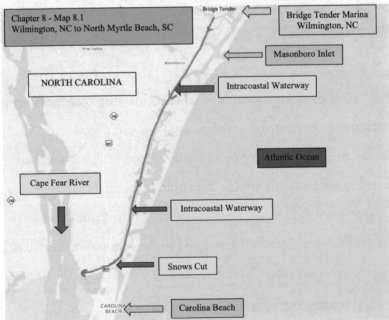

Chapter 8 - Map 8.1
Wilmington, NC to North Myrtle Beach, SC

Bridge Tender Marina
Wilmington, NC

Masonboro Inlet

NORTH CAROLINA

Intracoastal Waterway

Atlantic Ocean

Cape Fear River

Intracoastal Waterway

Snows Cut

Carolina Beach

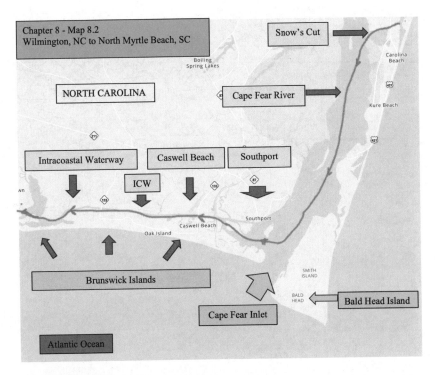

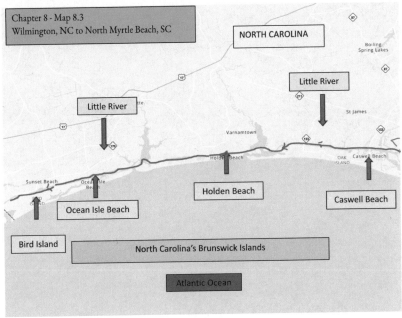

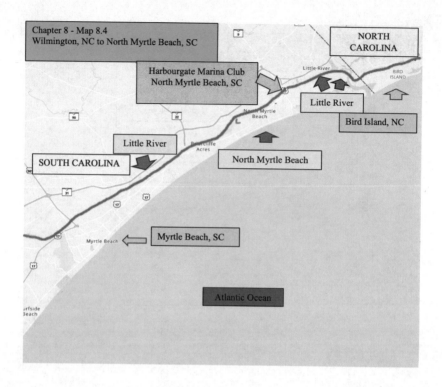

TWELVE BRIDGES TO CROSS

"Golden bridge, silver bridge or diamond bridge;
it doesn't matter! As long as the bridge takes you
across the other side, it is a good bridge!"

—*Mehmet Murat Ildan*

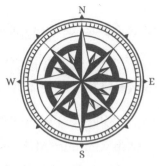

November 11, 2022

Harbourgate Marina
North Myrtle Beach, South Carolina
To
Harborwalk Marina
Georgetown, South Carolina

We left Harbourgate Marina, North Myrtle Beach, South Carolina, and headed to Georgetown's Harborwalk Marina in South Carolina. It would be a long day; we were heading south against wind and rain that was currently heading north. The distance of this trip was going to be about fifty nautical miles (sixty land miles). This sixty-mile stretch of white sandy beaches, known as "the Grand Strand," extends from Little River, South Carolina to Georgetown, South Carolina. This vast summer playland harbors everything from deep-sea fishing to shopping in little boutiques and flea markets. Gourmet delights are there for the tasting, and an expansive boardwalk creates memorable family fun.

Though only half the distance we typically planned to travel in a day, we knew that being on the periphery of Hurricane Nicole would impede our progress. Thus, we planned a more conservative distance in case bad weather or unexpected obstacles hindered us.

After consulting with Captain Mike, docked only a short distance north of us, we arranged to meet outside the Harbourgate Marina. Once we had a visual of *The Matrix*, we would pull out of Harbourgate Marina and go through the Captain Archie Neil "Poo" McLauchlin Bridge at mile marker 347.3, the first of twelve bridges along this stretch. I have to say that I find some of those bridge names quite amusing. "Poo" bridge—rather funny, if you ask me! This bridge has quite a bit of traffic, causing congestion through and around it, but that day, it was far lighter than usual because of the weather. The bridge was open, and we made our passage through, making it easy to keep in line with Captain Mike.

The *Sea Scape* traveled about ten knots per hour without creating any wake. After the bridge, we saw a beautiful golf course with low-cut, sweet green grass and beautiful pampas grass. We could tell it was windy without even checking at our Garmin wind instrument. The feathery tails of the pampas grass did a magnificent dance in the wind. I have a fondness for the botanicals I see along my journeys and always want to know more about where and how they exist. I found those pampas exceptionally beautiful just swaying in the breeze!

We also saw homes lining the banks, each with an extended dock. At the end of each dock were porch-like covered sitting areas; such a serene space to sit and watch the world float by.

Further on, we spotted condominium buildings, marinas, and even business buildings along the way. In the distance, we recognized old pilings used to support docks from the past, some barely peeking out, left to rot within the water like ghosts from another era. We were still traveling through North Myrtle Beach, and though the skies lay heavy with cumulonimbus clouds, no rain had yet fallen there. However, we knew we would meet the heavy rain falling south of us. A little further down the ICW, we encountered bridge number two, the Robert Edge Parkway Bridge, at mile marker 349.52, only 1.8 nautical miles down the ICW, a fixed bridge that was straightforward to maneuver through.

Bridge number three, the Conway Bridge, was 6.4 nautical miles ahead of us at mile marker 355.5, standing sixty feet tall with a horizontal stretch of 110 feet. Fortunately, the *Sea Scape* only needed twenty-seven feet of clearance. If you are a golfer, consider including nearby Arcadian Shores, in the heart of Myrtle Beach, a semi-private golf club, to your vacation list. This beautiful golf club was empty due to the weather, but I'm sure it teems with excitement on a sunny day.

Two nautical miles down the ICW, we approached our next bridge, the Grand Dunes Bridge, at mile marker 357.5. This fixed bridge with a sixty-five-foot vertical clearance and a horizontal span of 220 feet offered us plenty of room to slide on through. The Grand Dunes area of Myrtle Beach is appealing to many, with its luxury development for fifty-five-plus seniors, lavish first-class hotels with water parks, and golf courses that call every golf enthusiast's name—something for everyone. The Grand Dunes Golf Course is a top-rated public golf course with five holes along the ICW. Though most homes we passed were charming if more or less ordinary, we soon came along a swath of homes that were beyond outstanding. Homes built of impressive, prestigious materials stood outlined in stone and cedar, with manicured lawns and gracious gardens that acted as the finishing touch, as does a fine piece of jewelry for a woman's outfit. Their construction appeared to spare little. I do not play golf; I boat, but if I did golf, I'd have to consider the Grand Dunes area for retirement! What a beautiful place to live!

Another three miles down the IWC is bridge number six, the Grissom Parkway Bridge, a fixed bridge at mile marker 360.5. You may be wondering, *Why so many bridges?* The Grand Strand, which encompasses the Myrtle Beach area, is a mecca for visitors from all regions of the country. Many roads come into the Grand Strand, and many bridges cross the ICW to reach the Atlantic Ocean shores that grace this strand. The Grissom Parkway Bridge is near the Myrtle Beach International Airport and thus, sees its share of heavy traffic.

The Grissom Parkway Trail, an easy route suited to all types of bikers, runners, and walkers, offers a well-designed, thirteen-mile bike trail, but it is my understanding that since it is next to the highway, noise is an issue. I do like to bike but prefer to do so in a quiet secluded area—somewhere serene and peaceful.

Mile marker 364.4 brings us to bridge number seven, the SCL Railroad Bridge, only 3.9 miles down the ICW since our last bridge. This bascule bridge is normally open and stands just before bridge number eight, the U.S. Route 501 Bridge, a fixed bridge with a sixty-five-foot vertical measurement and a ninety-foot spread. The two bridges are so close together that they have the same mile marker: 364.4, with bridge number eight immediately following bridge number seven. The SCL Railroad Bridge was originally constructed in 1890 with the last update in 1930. It looked old and tired, sort of like how I was beginning to feel! Maybe I was just hungry! First Mate Lauri fixed something for us to eat. I was glad when we got through those two bridges. It amazed me how closely together they had been built.

Bridge number nine, the Fantasy Harbour Bridge, at mile marker 366.4, sits only one nautical mile past the U.S. Route 501 Bridge. This area of the Grand Strand, on the southern end of Myrtle Beach, has some of the most reasonably priced hotels. A great option for families on a budget and not far from the Myrtle Beach Boardwalk, located at the end of Route 501, a place all kids want to visit! I don't know one kid who does not like the beach or boardwalk! My parents moved from Brooklyn to New Jersey, where I lived for a major portion of my childhood. As a kid, I loved building sand castles and watching the ocean's waves come in and out. New Jersey has some of the best beaches and boardwalks in the country, each with its own special flavor. Cape May is Victorian, for example, and Wildwood is rooted in the sixties. Welcome to Asbury Park—we all know Bruce Springsteen who made it there! And lest we forget, those crazy kids vacationing in Seaside Heights who starred in the TV show *Jersey Shore*. A small state with a lot of hutzpah! Parts of the Carolinas that I've seen remind me of the Jersey Shore in its beginning stages.

After passing Myrtle Beach, we saw no homes but rather vegetation composed of scrub pine, Virginia creeper vines, and other wild plants along the banks, along with tiny, little fan-like palm trees. That day, we only spotted a few boats traveling down the ICW, probably because they feared the bad weather coming. We only saw an occasional catamaran.

We were getting closer to bridge number ten, the Socastee Swing Bridge, at mile marker 371.0, only 4.9 miles south of the U.S. Route 501 Bridge. This bridge in a small way reminds me of the Lower Trenton Bridge connecting Trenton, New Jersey to Pennsylvania. In 1910, the Trenton Chamber of Commerce held a contest for a slogan, which they would put in lights on the side of the bridge. The winning slogan still graces the side of this bridge and every night lights the sky with the slogan "Trenton Makes and the World Takes" in dedication to the number of factories that produce goods shipped to many U.S. cities but especially the China produced by Lenox Corporation. This is the same China used by presidents in the White House. The Socastee Swing Bridge, though much smaller than its cousin in Trenton, shares some similarities in its steel features.

Immediately following the Socastee Swing Bridge was bridge number eleven, the Socastee Highway Bridge, a fixed bridge at mile marker 371.3, only three-tenths of a nautical mile past the Socastee Swing Bridge's location. We knew we had to hurry to make the Socastee Swing Bridge's opening on time. In addition, looking at our Navionics map, we realized that the Socastee Swing Bridge would not open with sustained winds of over twenty miles an hour. Concerned that due to the upcoming storm, conditions would deteriorate further, we had to get through the Socastee Swing Bridge immediately. Otherwise, we feared we would find no refuge for that night and be stuck there in the interim. I did not want to think about what the consequences of that might be.

We switched to channel nine on our VHF radio, the hailing channel for all bridges along the ICW. We spoke to the bridge operator and gave him notice that we were very near. We reached the Socastee Swing Bridge, which he held open for us. We thanked him and our lucky stars and proceeded through the Socastee Highway Bridge, with its sixty-five-foot clearance, without any problems.

One nautical mile past the Socastee Highway Bridge, we encountered bridge number twelve, the Carolina Bays Parkway Bridge, at mile marker 372.3, which took us under South Carolina Highway 31. This fixed bridge has a height of sixty-five feet, which we cruised under with no problems. We were almost there!

Past the Carolina Bays Parkway Bridge, the waterway twists and turns, so you need to pay close attention to your navigational maps. As you head southward, you pass the Waccatee Zoological Farm just before Enterprise Landing. This landing, maintained by the Coast Guard Auxiliary, has two boat ramps, a floating dock, and provides life jackets to borrow. It is just past here that both the Socastee River and the ICW join the Waccamaw River.

We reached the Waccamaw River at approximately eleven that morning. The river looked much like the Pasquotank River when leaving the Dismal Swamp Canal in Virginia rather than the Alligator-Pungo River Canal. Pine trees and other vegetation heavily lined both banks of the river, which proved a bit more tortuous than the Pasquotank River, so we paid closer attention to what was in the water and who may be coming up north around the bend. Fortunately, hardly any boats were traveling that day due to the hurricane.

As we traveled on the Waccamaw River, Sarah, my first mate

Lauri's daughter, who loves following the weather, sent pictures of what was happening in Florida. The latest effects of Nicole were especially on display in one picture she took of a dock cut off from itself on the Florida coast. Those pictures helped keep us on our toes. We still did not know what to expect.

It was nearing lunchtime, and I drove the boat while Lauri prepared our lunch. Once the food was ready, she brought our meal to the pilothouse through the interior stairwell. As earlier noted, the convenience of this connection on the *Sea Scape* makes it possible to get a meal from the galley piping-hot to the pilot house. The person who designed the boat deserves multiple kudos! We ate in the pilothouse so that we could continue the voyage unimpeded.

Traveling down the Waccamaw River, we spotted a few marinas. When we arrived at Woodville Island, about halfway down the Waccamaw River, the weather changed. It started raining heavily. When we saw the river overflowing the banks, we knew we needed to be cautious. This took all our concentration. A third of the length of the trees we'd previously seen growing on the river's banks were now underwater. It looked as if those trees were growing from the river. What an unbelievable sight, and even a little scary at times! Thankfully, we were about an hour and a half away from Harborwalk Marina in Georgetown. We knew it would be a challenging period, and it was. We kept our eyes peeled for floating debris and paid close attention to all our navigational data. Another exhausting ride!

As we approached the marina from the Waccamaw River, we turned starboard onto the Sampit River and, after a very short distance, noticed how tranquil things turned even though it was still raining. Harborwalk Marina is tucked away from the river in a cove resembling a bay, which protects it from the ravages of the weather. It has an island on one side and the town of Georgetown on the other. We entered the marina at around 2:30 that afternoon with sighs of relief. Ahh!

Harborwalk Marina is beautiful, quaint, and well-maintained, with an excellent staff. Content to have gotten there without any significant events, we slowly approached the dock and tied our lines. The marina's location protected the boat from the wind, so we did not double-tie our lines.

There were also a few sailboats anchored on buoys close to

the entrance. Harborwalk Marina has free city water, Wi-Fi, cable television, showers, restrooms, a captain's lounge, and a laundry facility. Stationary pump-out and 30/50/100-amp services were available for a nominal fee. Ahh—all the comforts of home! We all took a deep breath, thankful we had finally arrived.

It was early in the day. The weather had lightened, and we all wanted to go out and walk around, stretch our legs, and see the sights in this picturesque, charming town. We were right in the heart of the historic district, so we walked up the street, and our first encounter, only a block away, was the Rice Museum. Here, we learned the importance of rice and indigo and how they saved Georgetown. As the leading grower of indigo during the Revolutionary War, Georgetown supplied it to the British so they could dye their uniforms. After Charleston, Georgetown became the second most crucial point of entry. At that time, Georgetown also supplied half the rice used in the United States and exported more rice to foreign ports than any other city. Who would have thought that rice and indigo could save a city?

After the Rice Museum, we walked three blocks further and visited the Kaminski House Museum, a typical low-country, single house of the mid-eighteenth century. It was a stunning representation of a low-country antebellum Georgian-style house. Though we have all heard the term low-country, we quickly learned exactly what it signified, namely, the area below the fall line where the upland region and the coastal plain meet. But the low country includes much more than the land's topography. It has a culture all its own, which stems from the popular culture of the African Gullah Geechee people. Those enslaved people brought the use of rice and seafood, as well as the art of basket-making, to the low-country culture. Georgetown offers a museum dedicated to their contributions. Unfortunately, we had no time to visit it, but we enjoyed some of the food.

The Kaminski House, listed in the National Register of Historic Places, is a single-family home built on the bluffs overlooking the Sampit River. As you stand on its porch, you can understand the beauty of its existence. Its style of architecture, Georgian, was designed after homes in Barbados, which also influenced home design in Charleston, and was intended to capture the breeze to cool the house and its occupants. Of course, as with many low-country houses, it boasts beautiful porches and a grass lawn from the front of the house to the street. Georgetown is the third oldest city in South Carolina and effortlessly fits the definition of low-country beauty.

It was near dusk by then, and since we were all getting hungry, we decided to celebrate temporarily escaping the wrath of Hurricane Nicole by dining at a charming little restaurant on the water called Big Tuna, only two blocks from the marina. The food was delicious. Captain Mike enjoyed the whole flounder, Andrew had the tuna bites, Lauri ordered the grouper, and I chose crab cakes, all washed down with a few beers. The dining experience helped relax us, something we all needed. We hung out there for a while sharing stories until around nine, when we returned to our yachts to listen to the storm-related news and then to bed.

We knew that before the 9th, Nicole had made landfall on Great Abaco Island and, hours later, strengthened to a Category 1 hurricane and then landed on Grand Bahama Island. As predicted, it weakened to a tropical depression and was currently moving from north Florida to Georgia through Thursday night and into early Friday morning, with Western South Carolina predicted to see some impact. If all remained according to the weather prediction, we would most likely escape the full brunt of this storm, but until that was a sure thing, we would not un-cross our fingers!

OVERVIEW

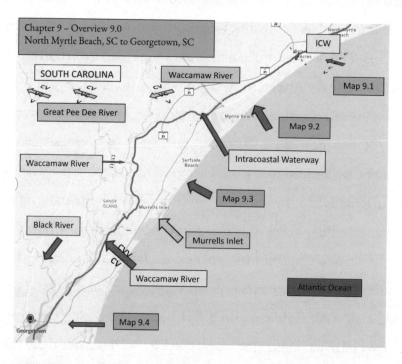

Chapter 9 – Overview 9.0
North Myrtle Beach, SC to Georgetown, SC

ICW

SOUTH CAROLINA

Waccamaw River

Map 9.1

Map 9.2

Great Pee Dee River

Intracoastal Waterway

Waccamaw River

Map 9.3

Black River

Murrells Inlet

Waccamaw River

Atlantic Ocean

Map 9.4

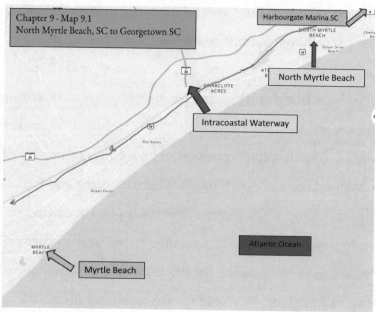

Chapter 9 - Map 9.1
North Myrtle Beach, SC to Georgetown SC

Harbourgate Marina SC

North Myrtle Beach

Intracoastal Waterway

Atlantic Ocean

Myrtle Beach

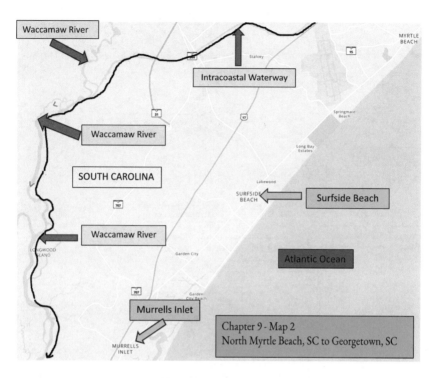

Chapter 9 - Map 2
North Myrtle Beach, SC to Georgetown, SC

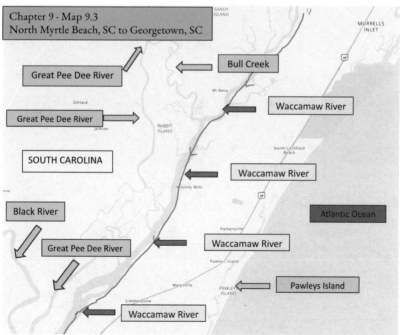

Chapter 9 - Map 9.3
North Myrtle Beach, SC to Georgetown, SC

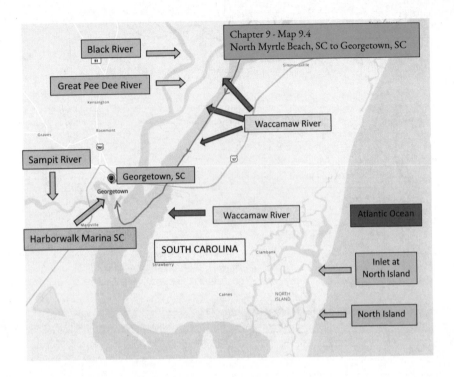

Chapter 9 - Map 9.4
North Myrtle Beach, SC to Georgetown, SC

Black River

Great Pee Dee River

Waccamaw River

Sampit River

Georgetown, SC

Waccamaw River

Atlantic Ocean

Harborwalk Marina SC

SOUTH CAROLINA

Inlet at
North Island

North Island

CHARLESTON, MY LOVE!

"I'm going back to dignity and grace. I'm going
back to Charleston, where I belong"

–Rhett Butler, Gone with the Wind

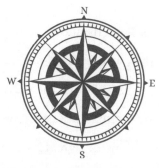

November 12, 2022

Harborwalk Marina, Georgetown
South Carolina
To
Ripley Light Marina, Charleston
South Carolina

The seventh day of the trip marked the halfway point. We left Harborwalk Marina in Georgetown, South Carolina, and headed to Charleston, South Carolina. Hurricane Nicole, downgraded at that point to a tropical storm, had started in the Northwest Bahamas, crossed over Florida, and then turned northeast. It had 970-mile, storm-force winds equating to roughly the size of Texas. Georgetown was approximately 350 miles north of the storm's center. I had felt some of its wind effects, but the immediate area only suffered minor storm damage. Lucky for us, the *Sea Scape* and *The Matrix* remained unscathed. We were very grateful the storm did not affect our vessels. The sky was blue and sunny, with only a few cumulous, benign clouds. The winds were minimal, indicating a beautiful day. Our sixty-mile trip to Charleston would have us arrive in the early afternoon, allowing us time to explore this remarkable city, especially the historic downtown area, a place of history, great food, and great atmosphere! I have been there before and have never tired of it.

The morning began as usual, with coffee and conversations about the day ahead. We headed to our boats, untied the lines, and met outside the marina in the harbor. The *Sea Scape* had to come about in reverse. Therefore, Captain Mike waited till we caught up. We followed the Intracoastal together because the ocean was still too rough.

We entered the Great Pee Dee River, formed by the confluence of four rivers: the Waccamaw River, the Pee Dee River, the Black River, and the Sampit River. The waters were wide and smooth in this area and easy to maneuver. Named after the native Winyaws who inhabited this area in the eighteenth century, this union forms the Great Pee Dee River's Winyah Bay. Cruising at roughly ten knots per hour, we followed the western channel. With Cat Island on our starboard side, we traveled approximately seven nautical miles to enter Estherville Minim Creek. Trees crowded the distant banks, and the creek was incredibly picturesque. Looking in the distance, it seemed as if the body of water would fall off to the end of the earth.

Our 4.9-nautical-mile trip down Estherville Minim Creek took us about half an hour, after which we moved down to Duck Creek. We wound around Little Crow Island, then Duck Creek, and at that point, we met the North Santee River, which we crossed. At that juncture, we entered and followed the Four Mile Canal with its exquisite display of greenery. Think about the last time you drove down a superhighway lined with beautiful trees and enjoyed the peaceful, tranquil ride and the traffic while humming along. Then, you will know what it is like to sail to Charleston, South Carolina, on the Four Mile Creek portion of the Intracoastal Waterway. It reminded me of a warm summer day spent cruising down the beautiful, tree-lined New Jersey Garden State Parkway.

This section of the ICW was as picturesque as a painting, with white puffy clouds positioned above our heads and tree branches reaching out to wave us on. It looked so appealing. I just wanted to take a deep breath and relax! The serenity and relaxing voyage on this water would calm any stressed-filled individual!

After a little less than 1.5 nautical miles, we crossed the South Santee River, where the waterway becomes known as the Intracoastal Waterway once more. The Francis Marion National Forest on our starboard side is a massive, 250,000-acre forest extending from the Appalachian Mountains to the Piedmont forests to the Intracoastal Waterway. No matter your outdoor taste, they have it. Trails for off-highway vehicles abound, as well as trails devoted to mountain bikes,

ATVs, and dirt bikes; horseback riding; and hiking. It offers plenty of paddle and fishing opportunities, rifle ranges, campgrounds, picnic areas, and even a historical wonder: a four-thousand-year-old, human-made shell ring. In 1989, Hurricane Hugo almost destroyed that forest. Over thirty years later, we are seeing the new growth grow and blossom.

At eight-thirty, we entered the area of McClellanville on our starboard side and the end of Jeremy Island on our port side. The same natural splendor continued as we headed through beautiful Charleston County. Gracing these shores, set back on the dunes, we saw the most magnificent-looking mansions. Surely costing millions of dollars, each mansion had its own distinctive style— each seemed more beautiful than the next. My first mate and I could not stop "oohing" and "ahhing" over which one we liked the most. A beautiful sight!

In addition to these beautiful homes, we had many sea-loving, black-headed seagulls in our vicinity, flying above our *Sea Scape* and providing us an excellent opportunity to increase our photographic skills. I grabbed my iPhone and took some beautiful photographs as they quickly scooped and dived alongside us.

Some dolphins played near our boat in this section of the Intracoastal. The Atlantic bottlenose dolphin can be seen up and down the Intracoastal in South Carolina; the best places in the area to view them are Charleston Harbor or the beautiful, exclusive

Kiawah Island, only about twelve nautical miles from the harbor. I could not even imagine how far they must have swam and wondered whether they were migrating south or pursuing food. Those playful sea creatures often swim near boats and are just plain mesmerizing to watch! We were lucky enough to have some next to us that day.

We then cruised through Island Cut, where we saw some lovely homes with attached docks and covered patios at their ends, much like the long docks we'd passed along the trip thus far. They were fine homes but nothing like the mansions we viewed earlier. However, because the water was very shallow in that section of Charleston County, the docks stretched out hundreds of feet—so that even the smallest outboards could dock. I dubbed them the ""Might Long Docks".".

About midway through that part of the journey, I spotted large, thick swatches of hefty bushes with beautiful white flowers. As we traveled the Intracoastal, I noticed these plants were mainly on the side closest to the ocean. I remember my fascination with similar-looking bushes in New Jersey called either Snake Root or Boneset, depending on the bush's form, but these were not the same. I wanted to steer close enough to identify them, but unfortunately, that was not possible because of the shallow waters along the banks. I called a florist to help me identify the plants because they seemed so abundant. I described the bush and its flowers to the man who told me he needed time to figure it out and would call me back. He did so about a half-hour later and listed out some names, but I knew none of them were the answer. I have good knowledge of plants and knew these did not match the names he provided. Therefore, I waited and did my research after we'd docked. Later, after searching the internet, I found that these plants have a few names: the Eastern Baccharis, Groundsel Bush, or Saltbush. They grow in the coastal Atlantic and Gulf areas of the eastern and southern United States. My curiosity was satisfied!

The next 4.6 nautical miles of the ICW are known by two names: Mathews Cut is the first section, and the second section is Harbor River. After Harbor River, the name returns to Intracoastal Waterway again. We entered Isle of Palms by midday, another of the perfect family vacation spots peppering the Atlantic coast. Adults can enjoy this island's golf courses; plus, there are a myriad of sports activities for the kiddies! It has a rich history involving early settlers and Civil War expeditions. Legend has it that pirates buried their treasures in the dunes and woods. Today, people still search for those treasure chests, but none have succeeded yet! With its six-mile-long pristine beach, Isle of Palms exemplifies the best of South Carolina's low-country living, with beautiful southern-style homes with docks and covered patios dotting their banks.

Cruising down the IWC, 2.4 nautical miles further, at mile marker 458.9, we approach the Isle of Palms Connector Bridge, a fixed sixty-five-foot vertical clearance with a 110 horizontal clearance that passes under US Route 17.

A short distance further, we crossed Breach Inlet and then cruised alongside Sullivan's Island, an island rich in the history of our country. Captain Florence O'Sullivan protected Charleston Harbor from the French and English during colonial times and used this island as a lookout and gun station point. Eighteenth-century enslaved Africans, enduring the middle passage, were first brought to Sullivan's Island before being sold in Charleston. Diseases such as cholera, smallpox, and measles infected many of the enslaved Africans and crew members aboard these ships. The government of Charleston established a strict quarantine protocol. Pest houses, short for pestilence or plague houses, held ill, enslaved Africans and crew members. The quarantine lasted for ten days before they were allowed to enter Charleston. Today, Sullivan's Island is called the Ellis Island for African Americans. Credited with processing 40 percent of the enslaved Africans, further research on Sullivan's Island has found that the numbers might be lower. Nevertheless, it was still a gatekeeper for many of the enslaved Africans who arrived on South Carolina's shores for sale in Charleston. Today, this barrier island is much like the Isle of Palms, with family recreation and beautiful beaches. Reaching Sullivan's Island told us we were very close to Charleston Harbor, and our excitement grew!

At mile marker 467.3, we approached the Ben Sawyer Memorial Bridge/SC 703, connecting Sullivan's Island to the mainland. This swing bridge opens on a signal but has complicated defined opening times. It is essential to check the opening schedule because it appears that it need not open during rush hours if the bridge master so chooses. We were not in rush hour, so we signaled, and our journey was unhampered.

One nautical mile further, we entered Charleston Harbor, an eight-square-mile inlet. Many dolphins swam along with our boat in that harbor, which only added to our excitement of reaching the marina with time to explore this extraordinary city. The confluence of four waterways, the Ashley River, the Cooper River, the Wando River, and the Atlantic Intracoastal Waterway, make up the harbor. The Charleston Inlet leads to the Atlantic Ocean. As a medium-sized port, it has public and private terminals, with the Ashley River side of Charleston Harbor being more industrialized. The larger portion of vessels sailing in the harbor are pleasure crafts and sailing boats. The harbor waters are wider and rougher than the Intracoastal, primarily due to the water that comes through the inlet. After Nicole's threat, the beautiful weather of the day had brought out many boaters, so we needed to keep our eyes wide open. This harbor remains part of the Intracoastal Waterway. However, that day, since huge volumes of water had pushed in from the ocean through the inlet, the entrance into the harbor was a bit rougher than the previous part of the Intracoastal on which we had just traveled. We came out of Sullivan's Island, then north along

Hog Island Channel and, at that juncture, turned west toward the Ashley River to our reservation at the Ripley Light Marina.

Charleston, the oldest city in South Carolina, is rife with history. The first example of Charleston's fabled history was on our port side. Located on James Island, we saw Fort Sumter in the distance. As many may remember from their elementary school days, April 12, 1861, saw the first battle of the Civil War, which took place at Fort Sumter. Colonists had built the fort on a sandbar, fortified with seventy thousand pounds of granite from New England. As a member of the newly formed Confederate States of America, South Carolina was fighting for its independence from the United States and saw the fort bombarded for thirty-four hours straight. The National Park Service operates the fort, and a ferry ride twice a day takes you across the harbor to the fort for an informative tour.

Closing in on our destination, we passed near Safe Harbor Marinas, a mega boat dock only half a nautical mile to our starboard side. This mega dock can hold vessels up to four hundred feet long, and we certainly saw a few! Wow, were they big! Stunning examples of some of the best there are—a sight to behold.

Ripley Light Marina is a small marina that, we noticed upon approach, already housed many beautiful boats. Once we arrived, my first mate and I took care of the usual docking duties.

We then headed over to the marina's office, where, inside, we saw a wall posting the names of the boats docked there. I got a kick out of reading the names of some of these boats: *High Tide, Inappropriate, Beyond Hope, Sea the Day, Undertaker, High Yield, Tighten Up, Redemption, My Three Sons,* and many others. You will often hear a great tale when you ask someone how they thought up the name for their boat. One of my friends likes to fish for shark, so he named his boat *Hammerhead.* Since he was in the construction field, we like to bust him by calling *him* Hammerhead! Another of my fishing buddies named his boat *Reel Love*—his wife did not appreciate that one! Another guy I know loved Billy Joel's song "Uptown Girl," and yep, you guessed it! He named his boat *Uptown Girl* and drove us all crazy constantly playing that song! But that's all part of the boating life!

After laughing about some of the names, we met up with Captain Mike and his first mate and headed downtown. Being an amateur botanist, I could not help but notice the first two trees we saw at the entrance to the marina. Charleston is well known for its palmetto trees and, true to form, two sabal palmettos stood at the entrance. Also known as the cabbage palm, these trees can reach up to sixty-five feet in height tall, from which round balls of fronds grow that produce beautiful, fragrant flowers. Thousands of them could be seen all around this town. The other tree at the entrance was a gorgeous date palm, which grows the fruit that is so popular to eat.

The harbor was close to downtown Charleston, one of the most charming and pleasurable downtown areas I have visited. Charleston provides free and paid walks, filled with southern hospitality, which are fascinating, informative, and picturesque.

There are so many things to do and see in Charleston that one could spend days there and still feel as if they have only experienced an inkling of the story this city has to tell.

My favorite Charleston sights are the gardens, landscapes, manicured homes, and fine buildings.

The flora and foliage enhance every aspect of their low-country living! Additionally, the architecture of those old, southern-style, picturesque, historic homes, dating back to pre-Civil War times, just seems to beckon!

There is nothing like The Jasper, a beautiful small botanical walk that holds some of the most beautiful tropical plants I have seen in a long time. Galleries and studios in the area house unique and stunning artwork. I could get lost for hours going from one gallery to the next!

The restaurants are also exceptional, thanks to their phenomenal, tasty, low-country Southern food. My favorite is Magnolias, and I believe it when they say they have defined Southern cuisine for over thirty years! Just scrumptious! They offer the types of low-country dishes one can only find in Charleston: fried green tomatoes, down south egg rolls, spicy shrimp, and sausage, to name just a few of their appetizers! As delicious as I found their low-country bouillabaisse with andouille sausage, buttermilk fried chicken with creamed corn, and cracked black pepper biscuits, my absolute favorite is still their bourbon-glazed pork chops, accompanied by red rice with kielbasa and low-country succotash! Wow, what a meal! I get hungry just thinking about it! I always return to Magnolias every time I am in Charleston and am never disappointed. That was where I planned for us to eat that night!

One of Charleston's most popular attractions is the Coastal Carolina Flea Market, an emporium of over one thousand vendors selling everything, including food, clothing, electronics, jewelry, and collectibles. If you like to shop and know your merchandise, bargain-hunting or shopping for unique collectibles at this emporium will make for a fun day.

Sometimes, listening to people's stories is even more interesting, and everyone there seemed to have one! While we were there we even discovered that there were three West Marine stores around town.

There was just so much to see, but all too soon, it was time for us to say goodbye to the picturesque town of Charleston, South Carolina, which had quickly become one of my favorite places to visit. I understand why some people who said they originally just came to visit wound up residing there. I did not want to leave either and was sad when the time came, but knowing I intended to return regularly made leaving that beautiful city a bit easier. We had a great afternoon and evening in the grace of that historic town. I look forward to returning to Charleston's welcoming arms, with its Southern charm and hospitable atmosphere.

OVERVIEW

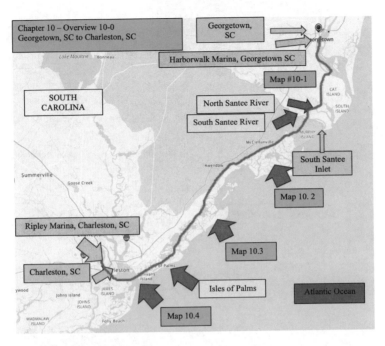

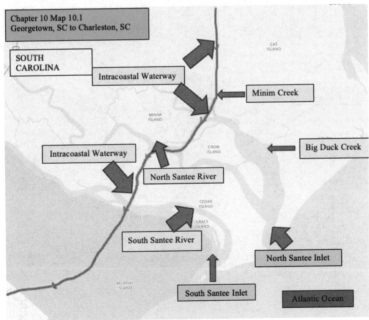

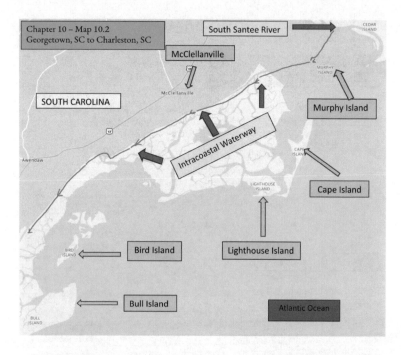

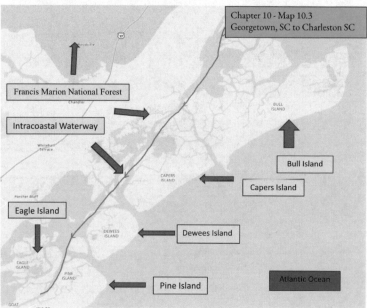

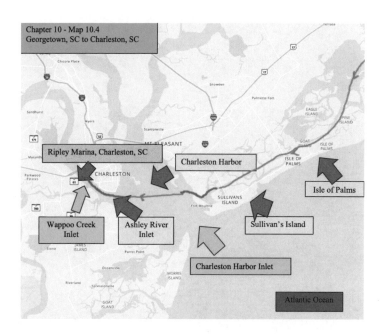

Chapter 10 - Map 10.4
Georgetown, SC to Charleston, SC

Ripley Marina, Charleston, SC

Charleston Harbor

Isle of Palms

Wappoo Creek Inlet

Ashley River Inlet

Sullivan's Island

Charleston Harbor Inlet

Atlantic Ocean

EMERGENCY!

"If you can learn to stay cool and keep thinking,
you'll figure out what you need to do."

—*Vincent H. O'Neil,* A Pause in the Perpetual Rotation

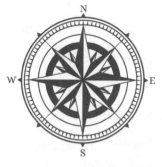

November 13, 2022

Ripley Light Marina
Charleston, South Carolina
to
Safe Harbor Port Royal Marina
Beaufort, South Carolina

The morning of November 13th was calm and sunny as we headed to Beaufort, South Carolina. As we departed Charleston, we looked up at the sky filled with low, puffy stratocumulus clouds, telling us we were in for a nice day. We felt the weather was with us and were ready to renew our journey. We came down the Ashley River and headed under the James Island Expressway Bridge heading west onto Elliot's Creek, a route that let us enter the long, snakelike Stono River. The coastline of this river was lined by dense trees but in some sections, homes set a good distance apart, each having a dock with beautiful patios designed for entertaining al fresco appeared. Outdoor sofas, bar set-ups, and large tables and umbrellas were ready for their occupants' enjoyment and to protect them from the scorching summer sun. We traveled this long, meandering river for some ten nautical miles as it swung around Sandy Bay, then traveled southward until it reached Rantowles, and then turned southeast, where the Stono River flows into the Wadmalaw River.

The entrance into the Wadmalaw is so wide that it looks like a sound. The waters were calm, and the winds were mild, which made me think of the phrase "the calm after the storm" after knowing that Hurricane Nicole had passed it. We continued following Captain Mike and *The Matrix* as he led the way. Suddenly, we saw that his boat had stopped in the middle of the Wadmalaw River. What reasons could have made him stop? Multiple reasons ran through our minds: *"Did he have enough fuel?" "Was there an engine problem?" "Did his generator fail?"* I immediately used the VHF to contact Mike. He responded that an alarm for the port engine had sounded, so he turned both the starboard and port engines off and was investigating the problem. He encouraged us to go on without him while he attended to *The Matrix*'s problem and would catch up with us. Captain Mike had a wealth of knowledge regarding boats and could usually find a solution to most issues, but engine problems can be serious.

Though it was Saturday, we thought marine services would be available to aid *The Matrix*. We assured Mike that while he was dealing with the situation, we would pursue a maritime service for help. We had just passed a major marina with a huge travel lift and were very impressed with its size. So, we assumed that this marina would most likely be able to help if open. We called them using our cell phones but to no avail. Knowing it was Saturday and many marine services might be closed, we felt uneasy but focused on contacting several anyway. Understanding that he had lost control of *The Matrix*, Captain Mike told us he would throw out his anchor to stop the boat from drifting with the current. We called BoatUS for a tow. They told us that to be towed in, we needed to have a slip reserved. We asked whether, for safety, they could just tow *The Matrix* to a marina's bulkhead, but they refused. I could not believe their response. It was unreal. They advertise twenty-four-hour towing service but never mention that stipulation. The company needs to change in my opinion. It is not how one should service the boating community or boats in distress, especially in light of safety concerns.

Being in our comfortable *Sea Scape* made us feel luckier, but we were very concerned about *The Matrix*. Traveling together on this trip, we had established a friendship and camaraderie and felt responsible for each other's safety. What to do? Captain Mike became insistent that we continue downstream. I trusted his judgment and knew he had a handle on things; otherwise, he probably would not have told us to continue. We were more nervous about *The Matrix* than ourselves because we felt helpless.

I discussed it with my first mate, Lauri, and we took Captain Mike's advice. We would continue downstream, hoping Mike could solve *The Matrix*'s problem and catch up to us, but only with the promise from Captain Mike that he would stay in constant contact. Captain Mike radioed us within twenty minutes as we continued down the Wadmalaw River and explained the cause of his problem. The cap on the oil dipstick for the port engine had not been tightly secured. He checked the dipstick and discovered that there was almost no oil in the engine, which had triggered the alarm. As a result, the port engine leaked oil onto the engine room floor. Mike attempted to clean the engine room floor but was out of rags. A complete cleanup would have to wait until we arrived at the marina in Beaufort and got some much-needed cleaning supplies. We prayed the engine was still workable. He added oil to the engine, crossed his fingers, and it started up. Thankfully, it worked!

Once we realized he was on his way, we dropped our speed to allow him to catch up. He cruised a little slower but soon reached us. We breathed a sigh of relief for them and were grateful that Captain Mike was able to resolve the issue. Mike's knowledge of boats was on target in that situation, and I was happy we were again making our way with *The Matrix*.

Almost nine nautical miles later, we approached the Dawho River, into which the Wadmalaw River runs. If you asked what I saw on the Wadmalaw River, I could not even tell you. As we came down from the adrenaline rush, we only focused on the water ahead of us and didn't even look at the shoreline. We were just happy *The Matrix* was with us.

Shortly, we approached the McKinley Washington Jr. Bridge at mile marker 501.3, with a vertical clearance of sixty-five feet and a horizontal clearance of 130 feet. This bridge allows you to cross under South Carolina Highway 174, which connects the mainland of Whooping Island and Edisto Island. The Edisto IWC Boat Landing is near this bridge and provides a launching site for those looking to go boating in North Creek and the Edisto River.

At around 10:30 in the morning, a quarter mile down the river, we arrived at North Creek. The weather continued to be warm and the skies sunny. On the shores, we saw lots of swaying marsh grass in the distance, the wind was mild, and trees lined the banks. We continued toward Jehossee Island and reached it around 11 in the morning. By 1:30 that afternoon, we entered the South Edisto River, which appeared very wide and looked more like a sound than a river. We then continued southward on the South Edisto River.

Here, we started seeing more boats. At one point, a man was driving a center console with a dog standing at its bow. Suddenly, a lot of thoughts ran through my head. It was a beautiful sight that can make one feel warm and cozy, but I was also concerned about the dog's safety. On a boat, there is always an opportunity for unpredictable events that can lead to a tragedy for man's best friend or even man himself. Was this dog so well trained that if his instincts had taken over, he would not dive off the boat to chase a bird or something in the water? Was the ride so stable that the dog would not lose his balance and fall off the boat? If he did, what would happen then? Could the owner dive into the water in time to rescue him? Could the dog swim to shore, which was quite a distance away? Taking such risks with one's best friend's life did not seem right

A dog is like a child, unable to help himself for the most part, and can be helpless in an emergency. Providing their dog with some sense of safety and comfort seemed essential to me. I would hope for them too. Such irresponsibility made me angry.

We have all heard the adage that an ounce of prevention is worth a pound of cure. Where was the ounce of prevention? My love for my dog would commanded me to act more responsible for its life. If I did leash my dog on my boat, I would provide it with a harness, complete with a floatation device. Having a dog there unleashed appeared to be not a well-thought-out choice and showed a lack of concern on the part of the owner. It was beyond my comprehension.

The law does not hold animals to the same standards as human beings. Therefore, if something serious happens to a dog, some might think: *"So what? It may be sad, but it is not a person."*

Accountability for the care of animals at sea is far less stringent than it is on land, an imbalance that should definitely be rectified.

Dogs need special care while on boats. Every pet owner who takes their dog on board should consider having special equipment made just for them. A dog life jacket is a must, as is a lighted collar that can help identify the dog if they are in trouble. Also, slip-resistant water shoes will keep one's dog from sliding over the deck. A pet ladder/ramp should also be installed so that if the dog goes in the water, they can get back on board effortlessly. Lastly, I recommend getting doggy goggles and sunscreen for added protection against the elements.

These accidents are often unreported to the law or downplayed in the media. Suppose the press highlighted the need to care for our pets when taking them on a boat. Raising the level of consciousness and responsibility would help avoid potential accidents. I hoped that as our travels continued, I would see more owners providing their dogs with safety precautions.

Further down this waterway, an unexpected thing happened a short time later on our voyage. How coincidental that another Horizon power catamaran, similar to the *Sea Scape* but only fifty-four feet in length, should cross our path to starboard! What a surprise—and almost like looking in a mirror! I was excited to see another Horizon almost precisely like my *Sea Scape* there. I hailed the captain of that Horizon on the VHF. During our conversation,

I found that he knew Richard Ford, the owner and founder of the Horizon Power Catamarans Company located in Fort Lauderdale and he knew many of the company employees I knew! Likewise we also both knew some other Horizon boat owners. My newfound friend of this catamaran was traveling much faster than we were, and we lost him a short while later.

As we traveled, I remembered what my old friend Jim always said: "There is no need to work the engines too hard." I've always taken that friend's advice and try not to steer the boat over two thousand revolutions per minute. I figure, no need to stress those beautiful Caterpillar engines just because I can. I am a firm believer that if I travel around eighteen knots an hour, I can conserve some engine wear and tear, as well as save on fuel at the same time.

The next section of our journey included several twists and turns as we headed to Beaufort. So we paid extra attention to our navigation system. We continued driving the boat southward through the winding South Edisto River and then turned westward into the Fenwick Cut, which led us to the Ashepoo River. After 1.6 nautical miles northwest, we turned southwest onto the Rock Creek, also known as Ashepoo River. At the end of this short distance (only 1.2 nautical miles), we turned northwest onto the main section of Rock Creek. When we reached a fork in the river, it was time to turn southwest on a continuation of Rock Creek, also known as Coosaw Cutoff. After another short distance of 1.3

nautical miles, we finally entered the Coosaw River. We traveled west on that river for nine nautical miles and then reached the Beaufort River.

As we entered the Beaufort River to our starboard side, we saw a couple of marinas filled with sailboats with tall masts. The river turned, and so did we, toward Safe Harbor's Safe Harbor Port Royal Marina. As we sighted the marina, we noticed two tall concrete bridges, namely, the McTeer Bridges, over the Beaufort River, allowing one to pass under U.S. Highway 21. They work to help steer the Sea Islands' traffic around Beaufort.

We finally arrived at the Safe Harbor Port Royal Marina, a

family-operated marina located directly on the ICW at mile 539.7 and south of red day marker 244 in Beaufort, SC. We hailed the dock master, Cathy, and asked where we would dock for the night. The marina staff guided us to our appointed docking space. They were very accommodating and polite, and the marina not only allowed for great views of the river and the bridges but also offered many amenities, including free Wi-Fi service, water hookups, ice, showers, a laundry facility, a pump out, a fuel dock with diesel, and a waterside restaurant. Additionally, there are four other restaurants nearby. Great marina!

The first thing that struck me was the long gangways connecting floating docks to the walkways. Their angle was all-consuming because the floating docks accommodated the river's changing tides. They were so steep that it could make walking difficult for anyone not used to it. The tide changes here are between five and seven feet, depending on the day. Those changes happen four times a day, about every six hours, when there is a significant difference between the high and low tide. Every time I see this type of tidal change, I think about the gravitational pull on our planet that causes these tides and the amazing effects caused by the interactions between the Earth and the moon. In a few weeks or months, I will be so immersed in my life on land that I will probably forget all I've seen and not realize how much I miss such adventures on this marvelous trip. The universe, wind, waters, and all of nature have always been alluring forces in my life. That is why I enjoy boating so much.

Once we arrived at our docking slip at Port Royal, we walked up the steep gangway, made it to the dock master's office, paid our bills, and began walking into Beaufort. We needed to find and purchase a few items for the remainder of our journey. The marina gave us clear directions to find what we needed. The most pressing need was more supplies to clean up *The Matrix*'s oil spill.

Located on Port Royal Island, Beaufort is in the heart of Carolina's low county. Named for Henry Somerset, the second Duke of Beaufort, it is the second-oldest town in South Carolina.

Colonists built the city in 1706 and laid it out around a fort built to guard against Spanish invasion. It holds prominence for its preservation of antebellum architecture. Antebellum refers to the years between 1812 and just before the Civil War began in 1861. The Civil War brought about the occupation of the Union Army, but Beaufort retained its identity! Seven major islands and towns encompass the Beaufort region: Port Royal, Parris Island, Lady's Island, St. Helena Island, Hunting Island, Harbor Island, and Fripp Island. Beaufort has been used as a location for many famous movies, including *Forrest Gump*, *The Prince of Tides*, and *The Big Chill*. The wedding scene for the movie *Force of Nature* was housed in the beautiful Joseph Johnson's house's front yard.

As we walked out of the marina's entrance, we first noticed an area filled with beautiful white pampas grass tails. A few more steps later, we entered what seemed like a tropical jungle with tall, thick, wide-trunked pin oaks; on their branches were ornate Spanish moss, dropping down like feathery spirals. Wow, I had never seen anything like it! Early Native Americans called it "tree hair." It was like walking through a veil, filling my mind with questions. Was this some aberration or something I had never seen before? As I turned around to my friends, I could see the amazement on their faces too. I would have to do some research to find out more.

I later discovered that Spanish moss is an epiphyte native to the United States, Mexico, the Caribbean, and Central and South America. The plant grows on another plant, gaining nourishment and moisture from the air around it, and is covered with tiny gray scales to keep it going through dry periods, which trap water until it can be absorbed. It has a gauze-like, translucent texture. This beard-like veil, with a flat gray hue, can change to an illuminating pale white depending on how the sunlight hits it. When the tissues plump up after rain, their gray appearance takes on a greenish tone, and as they use the water, they return to gray.

With its preferred habitat being tropical swamplands, Spanish moss can grow ten to twenty centimeters yearly once its seeds germinate. Not suitable for feeding livestock, Native Americans used it for dresses and American colonists mixed Spanish moss with mud to make mortar for their buildings—some of which still exist today. Dried moss makes good tinder for fires, and one can also make it into blankets, ropes, and mattress filling. Mattresses filled with Spanish moss stay cool on warm summer nights and when used as mulch it soaks up and retains water.

We continued our walk, which brought us along a major thoroughfare with many automobiles passing at high speeds. On

the right side of the highway, we passed an unimpressive, small, one-story wooden trailer painted pink with a red roof. A sizable number of people were waiting in line, which caught our curiosity. A large, old, washed-out, round sign with a lobster logo hung off the gable that read CJ Seafood Express announced fresh, raw local seafood. Our curiosity got the better of us, and knowing that this part of the south was famous for its shrimp, we decided to wait in line. We bought a couple dozen, beautiful, peeled jumbo shrimp for that night's dinner. We bagged the shrimp and carried them with us as we walked to the West Marine store.

We would visit many West Marine stores throughout our trip since West Marine was almost always reachable from the marinas where we docked. I am sure its corporate headquarters ensured its stores were built near marinas to capitalize on boaters' needs, whether that applied to powered vessels or sailing. The much smaller, independent bait and tackle stores in the area, which carried a limited variety of items, could not compete with West Marine. However, they were great for satisfying the needs of the local community. Often needing more time or transportation, we were prohibited from visiting those local stores for our needs. For the most part, West Marine provided many supplies, with one stop-shopping close to the marinas. Equipment such as clothes, mechanical parts, lines, anchors, and boating shoes were always available. If not, each of those stores kept on hand a thick catalog with various products a boater could order, which, from what I understand, could then be delivered to the West Marine store at your next stop—but don't quote me on that!

Captain Mike and Andrew, his first mate, did most of the

shopping in the store, especially for the supplies needed to clean up *The Matrix*. It was almost 6 p.m. when we finished shopping, and it was time to return to the marina.

We had walked quite a ways and were tired at that point from the day's events. We decided we needed some transportation back to the marina, but nothing was available. So we had to walk back to our marina, which was quite a distance. Andrew, the youngest and probably the strongest, carried most of the heavier stuff, and Captain Mike and I hauled the lighter items. Lauri carried the shrimp!

Our walk had made us hungry. Lauri prepared dinner for us back on the boat, as she had done so many nights. Captain Mike and Andrew went to work cleaning up *The Matrix*. She incorporated the shrimp with pasta and some veggies to make a delicious dinner and accompanied it with a crisp salad. We also had some excellent white wine. We all gathered on the stern deck of the *Sea Scape* at its inviting dining table and devoured everything. Not a crumb of her delightful dinner was left! We enjoyed sitting, eating, and relaxing after such a long trek! We all toasted Lauri and thanked her for the great dinner she had prepared, then helped with a quick cleanup and were content that there seemed no serious problems for *The Matrix*. With food in our bellies, we gazed at the river and the boats in the marina.

The sun was beginning to set, and as I listened to some classical music, I reflected on how the sun rises and sets every day, but so few of us actually enjoy it. When you engage in boating, you are much more aware of sunrises and sunsets, and that day's was a beauty. The sun sang out a symphony of colors as it descended, the perfect conclusion to our challenging day. Sitting there, I could feel my energy ebbing and my eyelids getting heavy. We all knew it would soon be time for bed and said goodnight. The day had ended well, and all was good. We all retired to our beds to meet the challenges the next day would bring.

OVERVIEW

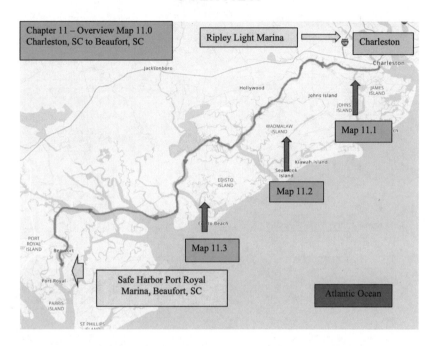

Chapter 11 – Overview Map 11.0
Charleston, SC to Beaufort, SC

Ripley Light Marina → Charleston

Map 11.1

Map 11.2

Map 11.3

Safe Harbor Port Royal
Marina, Beaufort, SC

Atlantic Ocean

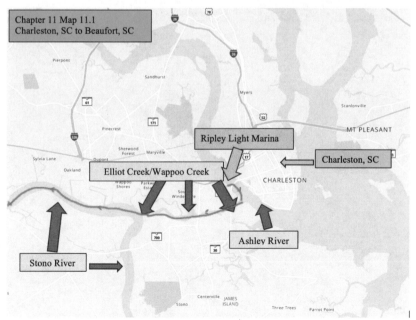

Chapter 11 Map 11.1
Charleston, SC to Beaufort, SC

Ripley Light Marina

Charleston, SC

Elliot Creek/Wappoo Creek

Ashley River

Stono River

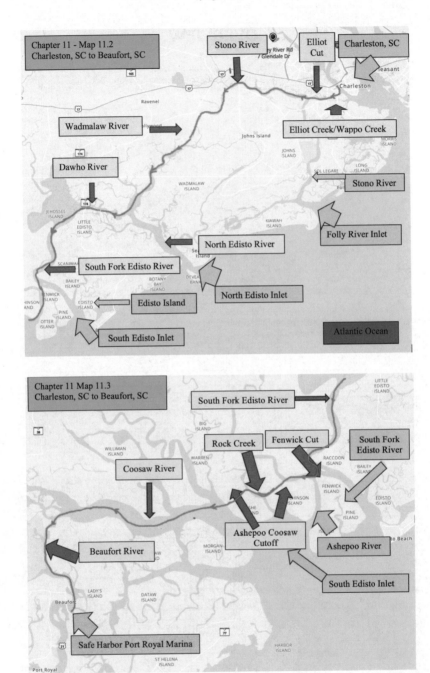

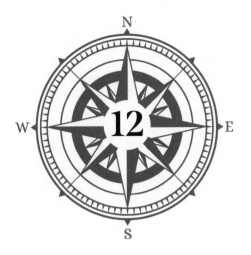

RIVERS, CREEK, SOUNDS AND INLETS! OH MY!!

"The moments of happiness we enjoy take us by surprise. It is not that we seize them, but that they seize us."

–Ashley Montagu

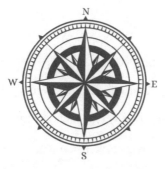

November 14, 2022

Port Royal Marina
Beaufort, South Carolina
To
A free dock on the Darien River
Darien, Georgia

We planned to leave Beaufort, South Carolina, and wanted to reach Jacksonville, Florida, that day, but we only made it to Darien, Georgia. The Atlantic Ocean was still very rough from the aftereffects of Hurricane Nicole. The wind was still causing gusts of up to twenty-nine mph, and the visibility was still down. Therefore, we decided to continue to Fort Lauderdale using the Intracoastal Waterway and other tributaries as much as possible.

Traveling the Intracoastal Waterway through Georgia became very complicated. Passage through the ICW in Georgia is complex, especially if you have never attempted the route before. A thorough understanding of this part of the ICW must be stressed more. Maps and navigational tools are great, but nothing beats experience. We charted our course using our Navionics application. The objective was to avoid coming out of the inlets into the rough ocean, and there were many! Our route was very spiral-like in some parts and zigzag-like in others. We took great care and remained aware of our navigation maps and the waterways in front of us. There was little time to enjoy the scenery as we had to navigate through an immense number of rivers, creeks, sounds, and inlets. My, my, it was complicated at times!

Trying to keep our eyes on the navigation system's information and the ICW was mind-numbing and presented us with some very thorny moments because of the many twists and turns involved. My neck was beginning to feel stiff, tense, and knotted, and my eyes felt like a yo-yo, looking from one piece of information to the other. Laurie was doing a great job trying to call out what she saw ahead, but with the visibility down, it was like looking for a house on a dark street with a tiny signpost. These complications caused us to underestimate how long this section of our journey would take.

Port Royal Sound Inlet was the first one we needed to be aware of and avoid. This inlet is directly south of Parris Island, the U.S. Marine Corps Recruit Depot. Parris Island trains some seventeen thousand recruits from east of the Mississippi River. They receive their grueling basic training on this eight-thousand-plus-acre island center. We could only see the striking green and ochre-colored foliage, but we imagined what was behind it.

From the tip of Parris Island, heading approximately four nautical miles southwest, our map showed us an entrance to Skull Creek. The entrance sat off our port side, at Seabrook Landing, along the northern tip of Hilton Head Island. Traveling Skull's Creek for about four nautical miles, we wrapped around the Pinckney Island National Wildlife Refuge and approached the

J. Wilton Graves Bridge at mile marker 557.5. A fixed, sixty-five-foot, vertical clearance bridge, it was an easy pass under.

We then turned to our portside and met up with Mackay Creek. That was when the twists and turns started for us. Keeping to our starboard side, we came to Cooper River and met up with Daufuskie Island, about six nautical miles away. After approximately three more nautical miles on Cooper River, it took a curve westward for half a nautical mile, then turned southward, which was where the name changed to Ramshorn Creek.

Just a little more than one and a half nautical miles south, on Ramshorn Creek, our spiraling path continued, and we turned southeast on New River for a little more than two and a half nautical miles. Our next move of only three-tenths of a nautical mile was onto Walls Cut, just above the Turtle Island Wildlife Management Area. Our navigation information told us to stay in the center of the channel on this narrow cut. At the end of Walls Cut, we needed to pay close attention again as we headed northwest onto the Wright

River for approximately one nautical mile. We turned southwest and entered Fields Cut, which sits between Hog Island and Jones Island, for approximately two nautical miles. It was just one turn after another in that area.

With another zigzag to contend with, our navigation system told us to cross the Savannah River and the South Channel Savannah River on this meandering journey. After crossing the Savanna River, we left South Carolina and entered Georgia, and we passed another state! Our navigation system directed us slightly northwest to take the Elba Island Cut, a peculiar cut that took us through three areas. The first section cuts  through Elba Island and Bird Island. The second cut involves crossing the South Channel Savannah River, and the third cuts through the Fort Pulaski National Monument in Tybee Island. Another batch of zigzagging turns to keep us on our toes!

Next, we turned northward onto St. Augustine Creek. One nautical mile later, we met up with the Wilmington River, where we turned to our port side. A nautical mile and a half later, we approached the new Islands Expressway Bridge at mile marker 579.9. The Sam Varnedoe Bascule Bridge, mainly deconstructed at that point, stood behind the new sixty-five-foot vertical clearance bridge that would eventually replace it.

Another two nautical miles down the Wilmington River, we approached the State of Georgia Memorial Bridge—U.S. 80, at Thunderbolt. This sixty-five-foot vertical and 120-foot horizontal bridge was another easy clearance. We continued down the Wilmington River until we reached another fork in the waterway as we spiraled around, with Dutch Island to our starboard side, then turned south at Skidaway Island's northern point and onto the Skidaway River.

We headed southwest through this river's snaky turns for approximately 5.6 nautical miles until we reached the Diamond Causeway Bridge, also known as the Skidaway Bridge, at mile marker 592.8. Some navigation systems said it was under construction, but it was completed when we arrived and is a beautiful, sixty-five-foot fixed bridge. Nice job!

A mere 1.2 nautical miles past this, we circled the southern point of Pigeon Island, and then one-tenth of a nautical mile further, we passed Marsh Island. Then the river became the Moon River. I wondered whether the song "Moon River" by Henry Mancini had been inspired there. The Moon River reached a curve, and my thoughts of the song quickly vanished. We began to head northwest, and the river became the Burnside River. When it reached the Vernon River, we turned south.

About one and a half nautical miles south, the Vernon River meets the Little Ogeechee River and continues as the Little Ogeechee River. One needs to be careful here. About four nautical miles south, the Little Ogeechee River, also known on some maps as the Vernon River, reaches the Ossabaw Sound, a large and potentially dangerous sound leading out to the Atlantic Ocean. So, with Little Don Island on our starboard side, we quickly turned west and headed to the area between Little Don Island adjacent to Raccoon Island, known as Hell Gate. There is little room for error there due to considerable shoaling in the area, so we carefully followed our navigational maps.

Heading westward, we entered the Ogeechee River. We continued westward until the first turn south onto the Florida Passage, with Ossabaw Island, also known as Queen Svetlana Island, to our starboard side and Levdahl Island to our port side. Our starboard side brought us past St. Peter's Island, and the Florida Passage broke out to the Bear River, which we followed slightly southeast and then south.

The trip felt like one long, winding river, creek, sound, or inlet needing constant attention, tiring my body and taxing my concentration. Until it was over, I didn't realize how tense my body had become. My neck muscles ached, my back was tight, and my head was heavy. I needed a good massage to loosen me up! Lauri and I constantly looked at the navigational maps and information, visually watched our direction, and kept in constant communication with Captain Mike! It was tough enough just to focus on where we were going, never mind always keeping Captain Mike in our view! Such a long, exhausting journey!

From there, we took the Bear River south for approximately seven nautical miles until we reached St. Catherine's Sound, which was home to St. Catherine's Inlet leading out to the Atlantic Ocean; the waters were rougher there. We guided our *Sea Scape* toward the southeast, past Walburg Island on our port side and onto the North Newport River, which hugged St. Catherine's Island, also on our port side. We caught up with the South Newport River about five nautical miles down the waterway. Then we entered another sound, the Sapelo Sound, with another Atlantic Ocean inlet, the Sapelo Sound Inlet.

The legendary pirate Edward Teach, better known as Blackbeard, is purported to have used this inlet. He scoured the Eastern Seaboard on his boat *Queen Ann's Revenge*, which held four hundred cannons and a crew of three hundred men! You can find tales of his pillages in many early colonial cities. He was finally caught in 1718 and met his end by decapitation. His boat was purported to have been found off the coast of North Carolina in 1995. His legend glamorized him, and he became the classic pirate. I think seeing the *Pirates of the Caribbean* movies really turned me on to pirate tales. Captain Jack Sparrow was some dude, and I'm sure the glamorization of Blackbeard influenced the script! The bonus was having Keith Richards from the Rolling Stones play his father was over the top! That was why I was surprised when we came upon the Blackbeard Island National Wildlife Refuge, a wildlife preserve dedicated to Blackbeard, directly to the south of us. We did not have the time to explore it, but Edward Teach assuredly lives on!

Approximately four nautical miles eastward, we entered the Mud River from Sapelo Sound, with Dog Hammock Island to our starboard side. Just past the southern tip of Dog Hammock, the Mud River meets a fork in the waterway. We went southward, turning to our portside, onto Old Tea Kettle Creek, which continues southward until the confluence of Old Tea Kettle Creek, the Duplin River, and the North River, just before the Doboy Sound. We knew that following the Doboy Sound would lead out to the Doboy Sound Inlet and into the Atlantic Ocean, where we did not want to go. The Doboy Sound Inlet is particularly dangerous, with severe shoals to avoid, so we continued westward at Doboy Island.

We reached the Doboy Sound, with Little Sapelo Island appearing on our port side. We traveled 1.3 nautical miles southwest on Doboy Sound and faced Doboy Island adjacent to Commodore Island. On the port side of Doboy Island is an entrance to the North River. We then took the North River for approximately one nautical mile until circling west and then continued south onto the Rockdedundy River for about half a nautical mile. We then turned west and entered the Darien River.

Those eight hours of our journey, which started at Beaufort, was quite an experience. The stress of all the turns and different waterways had affected us all. Captain Mike called me on the VHF when we entered the Darien River and asked, "Hey, Rami, you still with me? How are you doing? This has been one hell of a path, but we're almost there! I'm beat! How about you?" I told him I felt the same, but we had to keep going!

We had never traveled that path and tried to avoid any significant obstacles. Our main concern was running aground during most of the trip, which, thankfully, did not happen. That leg of the journey was like following a path along a maze or labyrinth, and we all hoped to make it to the end without any major problems! Furthermore, at times, we had to deal with undulating waterways, especially near the inlets, and various warning signals would sound and keep us alert and on our toes. There was little, if any, time to enjoy any of the scenery, but I do remember some lovely greenery and beautiful reeds the shades of ocher that seemed to whiz by my eyes. If you asked where exactly I saw those reeds, however, I truthfully could not tell you!

We thought we could reach Jacksonville by day's end, but none of us thought it would take so long. We had been so busy guiding our crafts that we almost forgot about reserving dockage for the night at our new destination, Darien. It was getting very late by then. Rather than calling around for a dock reservation for two boats, we decided to take our chances and go up the Darien River and see what dockage we could find. Little did we know that marinas in that area were scarce!

Since beginning our trip a few days ago, we were fortunate enough to have found dock space every night. That waterway did not seem overly crowded, so, being reasonable risk-takers, we took our chances, though we knew it was the more uncertain route. So, we proceeded upstream on the Darien River with our eyes peeled for a marina.

The Darien River had a strong resemblance to the Tuckahoe River in New Jersey, with its winding, narrow, shallow spots and shoals. The kind that we would have to navigate with a watchful eye and an alert mind. The length of this river is about seven miles inland from the ocean, also similar to the Tuckahoe in New Jersey. As a result of having navigated in similar waters and circumstances, I suddenly had a strong sense of deja vu. Maybe I was just tired, hungry, or starting to miss home!

We proceeded along the Darien River in our beautiful *Sea Scape* a few miles further. It was very late in the afternoon, and we were wondering what we would find on what appeared to be a rather desolate river. My apps told me little was available. How long would we ride the Darien River before finding a marina? It crossed my mind that this might have been an exercise in futility. I had yet to see anything significant such as an empty dock or a marina with a fuel station where they might allow us to dock.

About 6.5 miles later, we entered the outskirts of the town of Darien, located centrally an hour from Savannah, Georgia, to the north, and an hour from Jacksonville, Florida, to the south. It is the second oldest town in Georgia, with an approximate population of fourteen hundred.

The Golden Isles consist of Brunswick, Darien, St. Simons Island, Sea Island, Jekyll Island, and Little St. Simons. Spanish explorers seeking gold descended upon the territory more than four hundred years ago, discovering that the islands did possess what they sought. After that, the name "Golden Isles" was given to this stretch of beautiful barrier islands. Located along the Georgia Atlantic coast, these isles have been described as an essential tidal estuarine environment. In the spring, Darien draws thousands of visitors for the "Blessing of the Fleet," a festival to bless and honor the fishermen of the shrimping industry that dominates the Darien economy.

As we steered closer to our starboard side to avoid the shallow waters, our eyes caught the beauty of steel-hulled, blue shrimp boats parked one behind the next along the river's edge as if in a parade display. They were just fantastic. The sun reflecting off their steel hulls was a welcome sight. Finally, some humanity!

The sun was starting to set on the horizon, and there was

absolute quiet except for the humming of our Caterpillar engines. After admiring the beauty of those shrimp boats, I started wondering about where we and *The Matrix* could dock that night.

We could always drop anchor and keep our generators on or keep looking for that elusive dock where we could tie up, hook up, and get some rest. Where would our story end for the night? We followed Captain Mike up the river, making the trip easier.

I was getting a little tired and hungry and began thinking about dinner. All those thoughts were going through my mind when suddenly, ahead of us, maybe a quarter-mile in the distance, a beautiful, tall, beige concrete bridge—which I later learned to be the North Walton Street Bridge—appeared. Since bridges are prime locations for marinas, I held a glimmer of hope that a glowing marina would suddenly appear as soon as we passed under the bridge.

As if a miracle had just occurred, just before reaching the bridge, on the starboard side, a long, beautiful, clean, and empty bulkhead with a dock appeared. I felt it had been waiting for us and was inviting us with open arms.

But wait. I quickly realized it most likely was someone's private dock, not a marina. I'll be damned! That dock was brand-spanking new! Shining, beautiful, and sturdy enough for our two boats, just waiting for us like in a dream! It was open to the river on one side and surrounded by a fence and gate on the other. If we docked there for the night, there would be no getting to the other side of the gate. The fence was secured, locked, and too high to climb. Breaking the lock was out of the question, though I was tempted! Unable to open the gate, we were faced with the decision to either stay and chance it or move on to look for something better. We decided to drop anchor along the river and dock there for the night.

It was the brink of sundown. In about thirty minutes, there would be darkness.

There was no electricity on the dock. It must have been so new,

the owners had not yet installed the electricity. Therefore, we would have to keep at least one generator on to stay cool, which would create some noise. Would someone hear it and call the authorities? We also needed a generator for cooking since we were all starving and wanted to eat!

Our only hope was that nobody would come to evict us in the middle of the night. I talked it over with Captain Mike, and the decision was unanimously "Let's do it!" We tied the two boats back-to-back and got off our vessels at the edge of the dock to stretch our legs. I started snapping pictures as I usually do. Mike and Andrew joined me. Lauri immediately started getting the food ready, figuring that we might as well eat before we got chased away.

We got a better look at what was behind the fence from our current position. A large group of new four-story apartments or maybe condos sat nearby. Thinking it over again made me realize we might be trespassing on private property. We decided to go with the odds, figuring there was only a slim chance that someone would come out in the middle of the night screaming at us to get off their property. The apartments had no visible lights and all looked empty, but we did not know for sure. Everything seemed so new and quiet.

If someone did come, we figured we could beg for mercy and say we had an engine problem. If they were true boaters, we anticipated their mercy and forgiveness and would further ensure that we would spend the night troubleshooting our engine and then be gone at daybreak. We would plead for their understanding and say we were all but desperate. So, for better or worse, we stayed.

Tired, hungry, and with little patience left, we prayed no one would come that night. We sat down, ate, and then went to bed. We were mentally exhausted and knew we would need to leave lickety-split at early dawn! When I opened my eyes the following day, I had to stay still for a moment to focus on what had happened the night before. Gloriously, no one had arrived to object to our docking there. What a relief! We quickly got ready and headed out as soon as possible.

One day, we'll come back, of course, find a dock where we can stay legally, and then find out exactly where we docked that night.

We would have also liked to have extended our stay and gotten to know that quaint little town of Darien as we're sure it has a lot more to offer than the free dock we found!

OVERVIEW

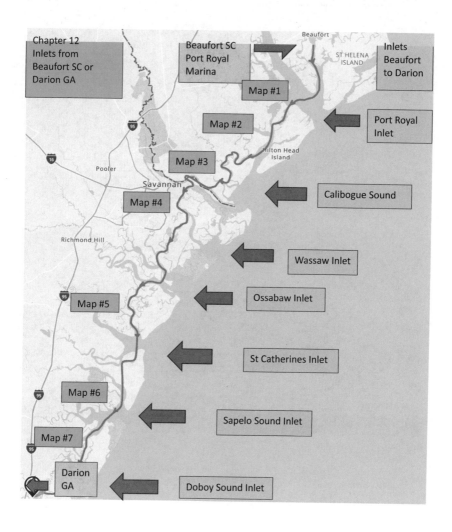

Chapter 12 Inlets from Beaufort SC or Darion GA

Beaufort SC Port Royal Marina

Inlets Beaufort to Darion

Map #1

Map #2

Port Royal Inlet

Map #3

Map #4

Calibogue Sound

Wassaw Inlet

Map #5

Ossabaw Inlet

St Catherines Inlet

Map #6

Sapelo Sound Inlet

Map #7

Darion GA

Doboy Sound Inlet

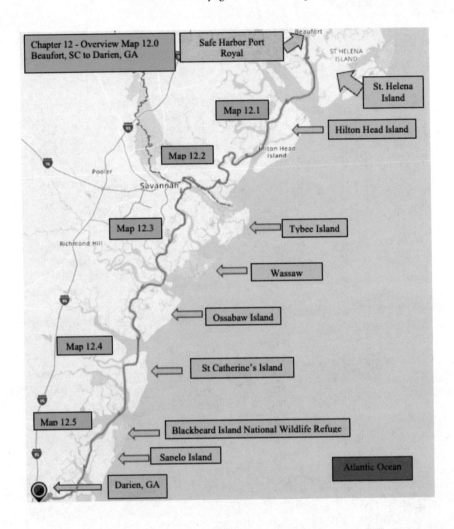

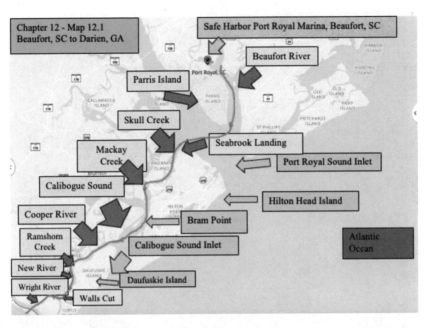

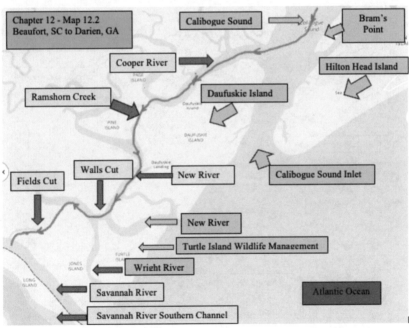

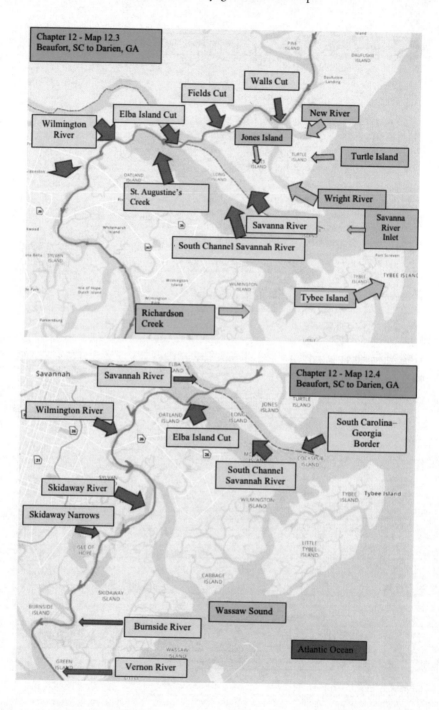

Chapter 12 - Map 12.3
Beaufort, SC to Darien, GA

Walls Cut

Fields Cut

Elba Island Cut

New River

Wilmington River

Jones Island

Turtle Island

St. Augustine's Creek

Wright River

Savanna River Inlet

Savanna River

South Channel Savannah River

Tybee Island

Richardson Creek

Savannah

Savannah River

Chapter 12 - Map 12.4
Beaufort, SC to Darien, GA

Wilmington River

Elba Island Cut

South Carolina–Georgia Border

South Channel Savannah River

Skidaway River

Skidaway Narrows

Wassaw Sound

Burnside River

Atlantic Ocean

Vernon River

Rivers, Creek, Sounds and Inlets! Oh My!!

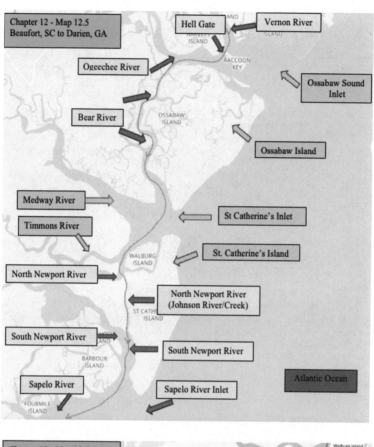

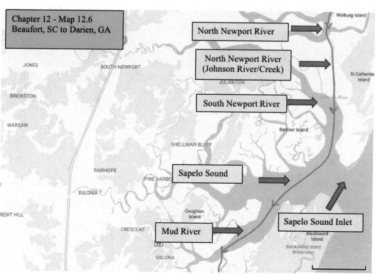

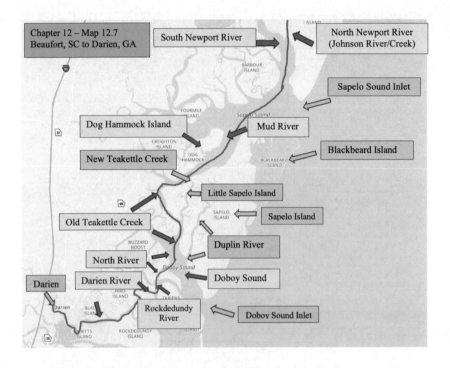

Chapter 12 – Map 12.7
Beaufort, SC to Darien, GA

South Newport River

North Newport River
(Johnson River/Creek)

Sapelo Sound Inlet

Dog Hammock Island

Mud River

New Teakettle Creek

Blackbeard Island

Little Sapelo Island

Old Teakettle Creek

Sapelo Island

Duplin River

North River

Darien

Darien River

Doboy Sound

Rockdedundy River

Doboy Sound Inlet

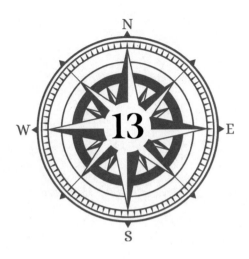

WELCOME TO FLORIDA!

"Hello! How's the weather in London?"

—*Mr. B.B. Webb, Engineer at the Arlington radio station*

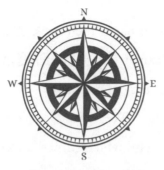

November 15, 2022

A Free Dock!
Somewhere near Darien, Georgia
To
Windward Jax Beach Marina
Jacksonville Beach, Florida

We started the morning with a cup of coffee and talked about our travel plans. After checking the engine oil, cooling fluids, and water for the sinks, showers, and the heads, we prepared to leave Darien. Keeping the music on kept us happy and grounded, so we turned up the sounds and left Darien, heading toward the Golden Isles of Georgia. Our journey that day was taking us past these fascinating islands.

We started heading east on the Darien River, traveling approximately seven nautical miles, and reached Wolf Island, a 5,126-acre national wildlife refuge that serves migratory birds and sea turtles, providing a place for birds during their annual migratory cycle and for turtles to hatch their eggs. Although you can drive your boat through its marshes, the beach is closed to the public to offer those birds and turtles sanctuary.

As we approached Wolf Island, we turned south and took the Little Mud River cut, which turned into the Little Mud River for approximately two and a half nautical miles. This cut let us out into the Altamaha River. We headed west on the Altamaha River for about two and a half nautical miles. As we approached Broughton Island, we turned southward to our portside, onto One Mile Cut, and followed the coast of Broughton Island into the ICW, known here as the Buttermilk Sound. Buttermilk Sound becomes the Mackay River, which we followed southward past Little Broughton Island.

Immediately to our east, we passed Little St. Simons Island, the first of Georgia's Golden Isles. This eleven-thousand-acre wilderness is a naturalist's dream. Little St. Simons Island is a private preserve, originally purchased by Philip Berozheimer, owner of Eagle Pencil Company. Established in 1856, the company manufactured legendary graphite pencils and writing accessories, and in 1938, added Eagle Prismacolor Colored Pencils to their catalog. This private preserve was Philip's family retreat for sixty-two years. He originally bought the island thinking that the cedar trees would be useful in the production of his Eagle Pencils but found the wood unsuitable.

Although he could not use the wood, he had such a strong fondness for the island that he built a huge house there and invited many of his business friends to vacation with him. Today, the only place you can stay on the island is at The Lodge at Little St. Simons Island. This lovely retreat is only accessible by boat and houses only thirty-two guests at a time. They offer a wide variety of ecological learning experiences that assist in understanding the ecology and conservation of the island. It is a true haven for nature lovers and supports the island's conservation. Being quite the amateur botanist and naturalist, I found this lodge to be an amazing place to examine flora and fauna. I only wished I had the time to stop the boat and stay, but our purpose was to make it to Fort Lauderdale, and our time was limited. However, that stop was definitely going on my bucket list!

Just past the entrance to the Hampton River, on our portside, we could see St. Simons Island, the largest of the Golden Isles of Georgia. Three miles wide and twelve miles long, it is approximately the size of New York's Manhattan Island. Both the British and the Spaniards have occupied this island. The English built Fort Federica, a Church of England mission. The ruins of this fort, made of lime, sand, gravel, and oyster shells, still stand today.

The plantation era saw many plantation homes built on St. Simons Island, which was known for producing Sea Island cotton, a long-fiber cotton prized in England. Hampton Point Plantation, the largest plantation on St. Simons Island, was operated by Pierce Butler, a signer of the Declaration of Independence. Mr. Butler engaged in the labor of over five hundred enslaved people on his plantation. Pierce Mease Butler, Mr. Butler's grandson, inherited the plantation. He and his wife's frivolous spending created an enormous debt, and as a solution, they decided to sell all the enslaved human beings on the plantation. The 1859 sale of 429 enslaved humans brought them some three hundred thousand dollars, equaling over eleven million dollars in 2023. Making it the most extensive known sale of human beings in the history of the United States. It was labeled "the weeping time" for the tears shed by the families torn apart due to this sale of human life. This unspeakable deed left a horrible mark on the Hampton Point Plantation.

Another interesting fact surrounding St. Simons Island was that during World War II, residents of St. Simons Island got a scare when two tankers, the Texas Co. oil tanker, the *S.S. Oklahoma*, and the Standard Oil tanker, the *S.S. Esso Baton Rouge*, were torpedoed by German U-boats, not far off the shores of St. Simons. In response, President Franklin Roosevelt had the U.S. Navy employ a convoy of ships to protect the area. Round-the-clock protection sent a clear message to the Germans, and St. Simons' residents rested a little easier.

St. Simons Island still has an outstanding reputation for such a small and relatively unknown island. While getting gas, I chatted with a fellow who told me about the Golden Isles of Georgia. He said that if I had a chance, I should go to the Southern Soul Barbeque on St. Simons Island for the best barbeque ribs I would ever taste! When I can explore more, I will definitely try it.

As we continued on the Mackay River, we saw the marsh and woodlands of the northern side of the island. Further down, the southern end sharply contrasted with its residential homes and commercial enterprises. Just by looking at the environment, we knew this was the land of sunny summer family vacations.

Eleven nautical miles down the Mackay River from the Buttermilk Sound, we entered the Brunswick River, which flows into St. Simons Sound. Just south of us, the northern tip of Jekyll Island faced us. Our navigation maps told us that the Jekyll Creek, also known as the Jekyll River, cuts through the center of Jekyll Island. We knew that was our destination. Four miles across the sound, we entered Jekyll Creek. Very importantly, this cut saved us from going out into the waters of the Atlantic.

According to the locals who live in this area, trying to get through this cut during the highest tide possible is vital to avoid getting grounded. In 2019, Jekyll Creek was dredged to only seventy-five feet, half the standard depth of 150 feet. They told us to keep our boat in the middle of the narrow channel and not to deviate more than twenty feet. Lucky for us, we were still in high tides as we approached it. We proceeded through the cut with our eyes glued to the sounder lest we run aground. As we navigated through, watching the red and green buoys ahead of us, we noted items on the creek's banks probably left during one of those low-tide moments when crab traps and other things disappear and then show up days later.

Jekyll Island's storied past starts much like the other islands and inlets of Georgia's barrier island coast. Spanish explorers tried to settle it in 1510 but did not stay. Then, in 1562, the French wanted to give it a go, but they also lasted only a short time. Then, in 1733, British General James Oglethorpe attempted to colonize Georgia. He established the colony of Georgia, and Jekyll Island was born. Oglethorpe named it after his friend and financier, Sir Joseph Jekyll.

The late 1800s saw the establishment of the famous Jekyll Island Club. Members of the world's wealthiest families bought the island and established its use as their hunting and recreation club. Completed in 1888, the Jekyll Island Clubhouse became the summer playground for the country's wealthy industrial barons. Club members included the families of William Rockefeller, J.P. Morgan, William Vanderbilt, and Marshall Field. They all built, as they called them, "cottages" on the island, which were actually large mansions that would accommodate their families and their friends.

In 1915, the first transcontinental telephone call, between J.P. Moran and William Rockefeller, occurred at Jekyll Island. President

Woodrow Wilson was in Washington D.C., Alexander Graham Bell was in New York, Henry Higgins was in Boston, Thomas Watson was in San Francisco, and AT&T President Theodore Newton was in Vail. The call's cost was $20.70, which equates to $629.25 in 2023, and Jekyll Island made history!

But more importantly, Jekyll Island's most historically significant occurrence was a 1910 secret meeting over the Thanksgiving holiday. Six major players of the United States financial world made their way to Jekyll Island dressed as hunters using alias names to keep the meeting a secret. A. Piatt Andrew, assistant secretary of the Treasury; Nelson Aldrich, United States senator; H.P. Davidson, partner, J.P. Morgan Bank; Benjamin Strong, vice president, Banker's Trust; Frank Vanderlip, president, National City Bank; and Paul Warburg of the partner, Kuhn, Loeb & Co. banking firm were not there to ride horses or play golf. They ate their holiday meal together and then sat down to devise a new national banking system. Imagine, they gave up their Thanksgiving time with their families for that important event! I wonder if they had turkey.

One week later, they developed the Aldrich Plan and proposed it to Congress in 1912. Although Congress did not pass the plan, Woodrow Wilson later used it as a basis for the Federal Reserve Act, and thus, the Federal Reserve System was established. Beautiful Jekyll Island provided the setting for these great minds in banking and finance to think through a plan to stabilize our national banking system. What a great thing to do for the sustainment of this country's banking system. I wish I could have been the proverbial fly on the wall!

Jekyll Island was in full use until World War II. Its visitors were asked not to come during the stressful time of German U-boats, and the island never returned to its former glory. The State of Georgia bought it, and it is presently under the Jekyll Island Authority and is listed as a National Historic Landmark. Jekyll Island is another one of the Golden Isles of Georgia that I must return to enjoy fully. Those preserved buildings exemplify how the financial barons of the United States lived and are now a national treasure, holding the magnificent history of an era gone by.

Two point eight nautical miles down the Jekyll River, we passed under the Jekyll Island Causeway Bridge at ICW mile marker 684.4. It was an easy pass with a clearance of sixty-five feet and a horizontal width of 110. One nautical mile further, we entered the Jekyll Sound. The confluence of the Jointer River forms the Jekyll Sound, the Little Satilla River, the Umbrella Creek, and the Jekyll River.

We entered the Saint Andrews Sound approximately one and a half nautical miles further south. Little did we know of the notorious reputation of this inlet! Unlike the Saint Simons inlet, this inlet is shallower, narrower, and not well-marked. According to our Navionics and the Waterway Guide information we accessed, the Coast Guard removed the buoys because they did not want people using this inlet from the Atlantic Ocean due to the shifting shoals. Pay heed to any local information you can grab regarding this inlet! I am not sure what the risks would be for a small boat with less of a draw than the *Sea Scape*, but the Coast Guard does not even suggest that a boat our size use this inlet to get into the Intracoastal Waterway from the Atlantic Ocean. It is very dangerous!

The Satilla River joins the St. Andrew Sound from the west as ocean water enters St. Andrew Inlet from the east. The confluence of waters makes this body of water unruly. We closely followed the course laid out by our Navionics app and carefully crossed the St. Andrew Sound, heading toward the opening for the Cumberland River.

After crossing the sound, we entered the Cumberland River. Passing between Pompey Island on the west, and Little Cumberland Island, and Cumberland Island on the east, we passed the entrance to the Brickhill River, which then empties back out into the Cumberland River as it circles the Cumberland Island National Seashore.

Cumberland Island is another barrier island that has been nationally preserved as a wildlife center. The southern states deserve congratulations for taking wilderness preservation so seriously! The island, which stretches across nearly ten thousand acres, boasts of untouched forests and undeveloped beaches, allowing nature to unfold its glory. You can reach the island by ferry service for a nominal fee, and if you want to camp overnight, you may do so for an additional fee. Further down, we passed Stafford Island and Drum Point Island, two additional untouched islands.

At the starboard side of Cumberland Island's southernmost tip, we found the Naval Submarine Base at King's Bay, Georgia. This naval base was the home of Trident nuclear-powered submarines. It is currently under reconstruction to refit itself to house the new Columbia-class submarine, which it will begin to service in 2031.

Just past the submarine base at Cumberland Sound is the mouth of the St. Marys, the Jolly, and the Amelia rivers. The southern tip of Cumberland Island and the northern tip of Amelia Island form the St. Marys inlet. It serves as the border between the states of Georgia and Florida. We headed toward the western side of Amelia Island and entered the Amelia River.

Amelia Island, one of America's top ten best islands, is known as the "Isle of Eight Flags." Founded by General James Oglethorpe, the founding father of Georgia, it was named Amelia Island after Princess Amelia, the daughter of King George II of Great Britain. Amelia Island received the title of Isle of Eight Flags because the French ruled it, the Spanish (twice), the British, the Republic of East Florida (1812), the Republic of the Floridas (1817), the Mexicans, and the Confederate State of America. Finally, it settled itself as a member of the United States of America. Each country influenced Amelia Island's culture.

No matter what type of housing community you seek, you can find it on Amelia Island. Famous for its Amelia Island Plantation, a private community nestled in the island's natural setting, it boasts nine hundred single-family homes and twelve condominium units, and premier golf and tennis courts abound. So many activities are offered there, it could keep you busy all day.

Amelia Island's housing and daily living expenses are typically much higher than in other United States cities, but the sunshine and beautiful weather are free! Though they had evacuated for several hurricanes in the past, none has ever landed on Amelia. Few new buildings occur due to space, so homes are older and have a higher upkeep cost. There is little in the way of diversity, but one reward is that Florida has no state income tax, and much of Florida attracts retired individuals looking to live in a resort-like community.

Following our port side, we passed Fernandina Beach while on the Amelia River. Fernandina Beach is the first beach town we passed on Amelia Island. A bustling downtown area with a Victorian flair, it is surrounded by small and large homes with a distinct Victorian style. You can easily find some Victorian bed and breakfast inns listed as National Historic Places dotting the area. New Jersey is home to the famous Victorian town of Cape May, and Amelia has Fernandina Beach—both great places to visit!

We traveled approximately four and a half nautical miles on the Amelia River, past Fernandina Beach. The Amelia River scoops to the west and then south again, and then there is an entrance to Kingsley Cut, also called the Kingsley River. We followed the Kingsley Cut south for roughly seven-tenths of a nautical mile and found the Kingsley Creek Railroad Bridge at ICW mile marker 720.7. This swing bridge remains in the open position unless a train is approaching. Our "bridge angel" was with us, and it was wide open! Our navigation equipment told us this bridge had a strong current!

A mere tenth of a nautical mile further is the Thomas J. Shave Jr. Twin Bridges, which take you under the famous route A1A. If you have ever driven down Florida's Atlantic coast, route A1A is your road. It runs the entire length of the eastern side of Florida and ends at Key West, where you can see the famous mile sign that reads Mile Marker 0. The sixty-five-foot fixed Thomas J. Shave Jr. Bridge was an easy pass, and we continued through Kingsley Cut, along the coast of Amelia Island.

At that point, we saw a few small planes going in for a landing at the Fernandina Beach Municipal Airport as Kingsley Cut approached the South Amelia River. Although it is not labeled a sound, the South Amelia River first appears as a wide body of water, and then once you are at Amelia City, it narrows more to become more the size of what one expects a river to be. We followed the western coast of Amelia Island through this sound-like body of water, then entered the river. Our navigation tool took us safely along the far western side of a small island.

For those of you with a taste that tends toward a more modern backdrop, who like to sit in a lounge chair, applying your suntan lotion, and having someone bring you a cocktail, the southern end of Amelia Island is where you will find the Omni and the Ritz-Carlton hotels. Likewise, another place to enjoy those cocktails on land is on the southern tip of Amelia Island. This section of the island is sprinkled with luxury homes nestled in between the forest, sitting on the beach's edge, each with elongated boat docks stretching out like fingers into the water.

After passing Amelia City, we passed a small island and traveled two and a half nautical miles before reaching Nassau Sound. A half-nautical mile across Nassau Sound toward the west is the entrance to Sawpit Creek Cut on the ICW. We entered the cut. Otherwise, we would have headed toward the Atlantic Ocean.

As we noted before, depending on what map or navigational tool you use, those rivers and creeks may have different names, so we've included all of them. About one nautical mile south, the Sawpit Creek Cut meets up with Sawpit Creek heading south. Some maps say Sawpit Creek, while others say Sister's Creek. Almost one nautical mile further, the ICW follows along the western side of a tiny island and becomes Clapboard Creek or Sisters Creek—

whichever your map calls it! Following this route will put you on the western side of Big Talbot Island. On the east side of Clapboard Creek/Sisters Creek are Big and Little Talbot islands state parks, and ecological and historic preserves are on the west.

About a half-nautical mile south the name changes to Gunnison Cut/Clapboard Creek or continues to be called Sisters Creek. From that point, we traveled south on this path until we reached a fork for Fort George River toward the starboard direction. The Fort George River would take us to the ocean, which we did not want. So, we followed the Clapboard Creek/Sisters River on the fork's western side and traveled southward until we came to St. Johns River. The difference between rivers and creeks is that though both hold freshwater, a creek, sometimes known as a rivulet, is smaller and deeper than a river. Like a river, a creek is less likely to split into channels or branches.

After entering St. Johns River, we crossed the Chicopit Bay into Pablo Creek, a continuation of the Intracoastal Waterway. About one nautical mile south on the Pablo River, we reached the Wonderwood Drive Bridge at mile marker 742.1. This fixed bridge had a height of sixty-five feet and allowed us to cross under Florida State Road 116.

The day's journey was almost complete, with only two nautical miles left to go to our destination of Windward Jax Beach Marine. When we arrived, the marina did all it could to welcome us.

They explained that they had bought the marina in 2020 and had undergone major renovations. It had two hundred wet slips and easily accommodated the *Sea Scape* and *The Matrix*. Our welcoming agent gave us information on their boat and concierge services. The marina encompasses Windward Wharf, where we saw gourmet food trucks, fire pits, and retail stores.

We had been cooped up on our boats all day and needed to stretch our legs, so we toured the area on foot. Our stomachs told us it was time to eat. We did not feel like cooking and wanted someone to serve us. So we walked over to the Dockside Seafood Restaurant at Jax Beach for a quiet, relaxing dinner and made the right choice! The food was delicious!

We started with some appetizers because we were starving at this point. Captain Mike kept challenging me to eat some fried gator tail on the menu. I told him I didn't eat any tail or anything alligator! We ordered some peel-and-eat shrimp that were large and fresh with a cocktail sauce, to which Captain Mike added so much horseradish that it made my eyes tear, but they brought me more so I could enjoy it without the extra heat. The shrimp were large, cold, and cooked to perfection! Then the table saw an assortment of fresh seafood: fish tacos, fried shrimp and clams, grilled scallops, and fried, softshell crab po' boy. They came out with all the fixings, and my, we sure did have a feast!

After dinner, we walked back toward the boat, stopped at the fire pits, and listened to some of the musicians playing. Since it was November, the warmth of the fire was very inviting. Shortly after, we said goodnight. We knew it was time to get ready for our next adventurous day.

OVERVIEW

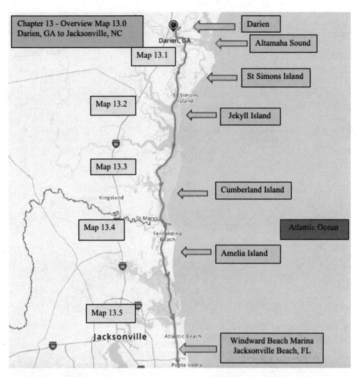

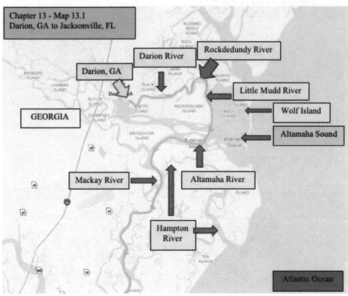

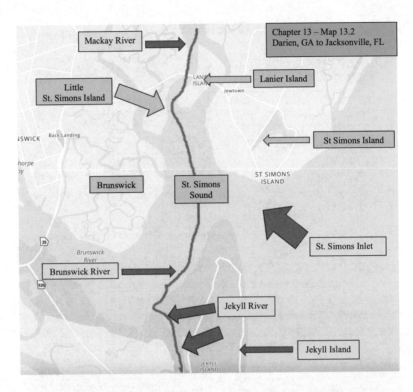

Chapter 13 – Map 13.2
Darien, GA to Jacksonville, FL

Mackay River

Lanier Island

Little
St. Simons Island

St Simons Island

Brunswick

St. Simons
Sound

St. Simons Inlet

Brunswick River

Jekyll River

Jekyll Island

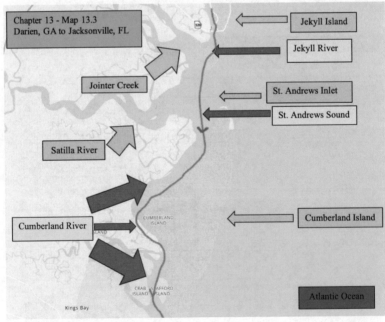

Chapter 13 - Map 13.3
Darien, GA to Jacksonville, FL

Jekyll Island

Jekyll River

Jointer Creek

St. Andrews Inlet

St. Andrews Sound

Satilla River

Cumberland Island

Cumberland River

Atlantic Ocean

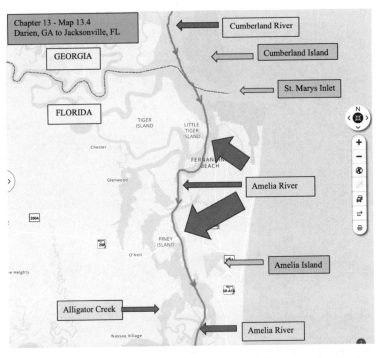

Chapter 13 - Map 13.4
Darien, GA to Jacksonville, FL

Cumberland River

Cumberland Island

St. Marys Inlet

GEORGIA

FLORIDA

Amelia River

Amelia Island

Alligator Creek

Amelia River

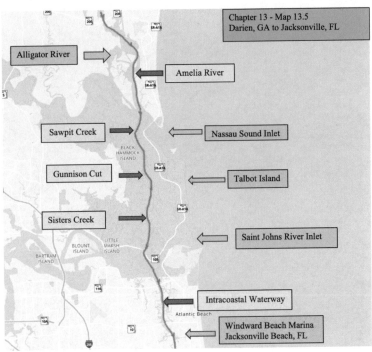

Chapter 13 - Map 13.5
Darien, GA to Jacksonville, FL

Alligator River

Amelia River

Sawpit Creek

Nassau Sound Inlet

Gunnison Cut

Talbot Island

Sisters Creek

Saint Johns River Inlet

Intracoastal Waterway

Windward Beach Marina
Jacksonville Beach, FL

OUR LUCKY DAY!

"Some bridges are so beautiful we wish them
to be our home!"

—*Mehmet Murat Ildan*

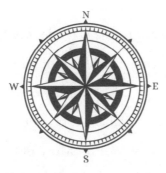

November 16, 2022

Windward Beach Marina
Jacksonville Beach, Florida
To
Bluepoints Marina
Port Canaveral, Florida

The ancient mariners had ways of keeping their lives interesting, one of which was to abide by the superstitions upon which they all agreed. Superstitions still hold a place aboard a ship today! You will never find a banana on my boat! Rotten fruit is an evil sign! Early sailors traveling from the Caribbean to the New World never knew of the ethylene that bananas emit and how it would cause other fruits in their transport to ripen and rot quickly. So they assumed bananas emitted some type of sinister omens. My first mate and I never eat our cereal with bananas. We eat it with strawberries!

No women on board was a sacred vow! The fear of arousing the men who would then forget their duties was real! Thankfully, in time, this belief went to the wayside. My first mate, Lauri, is a very able, intelligent, and capable sailor whose abilities are greatly appreciated!

Do you know the significance of a pig and a rooster to those early sailors of the New World? Most old seafarers embellished themselves with tattoos of pigs and roosters on their feet. Even Captain Jack Sparrow sported tattoos—twenty-seven of them, to be exact! Most old seafarers did not get that many, but having at least two was the norm. The pigs and roosters transported in wooden crates would float if a ship went down. Therefore, sailors believed that a pig tattoo on the right foot and one of a rooster on the left would help a sailor float to the water's surface in times of trouble. I have yet to gather my grit to do something to my skin that is so permanent.

Want horrific bad luck? Change the name of your boat without giving the utmost respect to Poseidon, god of the sea, and that's what you will end up with. Every sailor knows that Poseidon puts your boat's name in his book and gets upset when he has to make changes. Consequently, to avoid the god's wrath, one must conduct an official renaming ceremony, which goes as follows: Place the boat's original name on a slip of paper and then in a box. Then, burn the box and empty the ashes into the ocean on an outgoing tide while humbly asking Poseidon's permission to change the boat's name, thanking him for making the changes in his book and continuing to watch over your boat.

Another superstition we abided by is no whistling onboard, which sailors feared would whistle up a storm and disturb the seas. The most notable superstition is the saying, "Red sky at night, sailor's delight; red sky in the morning, sailors take warning!" Those old salts did not know that a red sky at sunset was most likely an indication of high pressure and stable air, and a red sky at dawn told of approaching storms and rain, but I did not see a red sky that morning.

I opened the door, walked out to the stern, and to my great amazement saw the most beautiful sky I could have imagined. Bright, light, pink, puffy clouds gave the sky the most amazing aura! Wow! The sky's color reflected in the waters surrounding the boat, like a kaleidoscope of pink and blue colors, enveloped by the dark reflections from the shadows of the oak trees surrounding the water's edge.

Scientifically, the phenomenon of a pink sky is called Rayleigh scattering and is most likely to occur at sunrise or sunset when the sun is at the lowest point in the sky. The rays must travel longer and pass through more molecules in the sky. A pink sky can predict the same stormy conditions as a red sky, but it is also said that seeing a pink sky with its cotton candy-type clouds is a positive sign. Still, it is also said to be a sign from the universe to follow your heart, trust your gut, and integrate your masculine and feminine sides. It represents a fresh start with new opportunities awaiting you. Upon gazing at the stunning display of colors in the sky that morning, I could feel my heartbeat throughout my body and just knew it would be a lucky day!

So, we cranked up the music and started our journey to Port Canaveral, Florida. We joyfully sang our hearts out along with the tunes we played, but we never whistled!

We started the morning at 6 a.m. after some coffee and a quick breakfast. A short distance away, a yellow-crowned night heron was atop a dwarfed pilling, enjoying the peacefulness of the pink morning. *The Matrix* and I pulled out of the marina, and we turned immediately south to our port side and went under the B.B. McCormick Bridge, which took us under U.S. Highway 90. This fixed bridge with a sixty-five-foot clearance, at mile marker 747.5, was accessible, and we started our new day heading down the Atlantic Intracoastal Waterway.

At this point, the Intracoastal Waterway is named Pablo Creek. Traveling down Pablo Creek for 1.8 nautical miles, we approached the sixty-five-foot tall, fixed J. Turner Butler Boulevard Bridge, which, at mile marker 749.5, takes you under State Road 202, another easy flow.

As we maneuvered down the ICW, the homes at Ponte Vedra were very similar to those in South Carolina, except their docks were an average length, as opposed to the "Might Long Docks" in South Carolina. At the end of these docks were gazebos with boat lifts that accommodated average center console outboards, mostly twenty to thirty feet long. The water in the Intracoastal was so very calm that even at the slowest speed, the propellers caused striking ripples in the water. Watching those ripples multiply, I fell into an awestruck state, thinking about how far they would travel, down, down, down the Intracoastal and into the mighty and vast Atlantic Ocean.

We traveled slowly through this area at seven to nine knots an hour. As we headed south past Ponte Vedra, we saw some exquisite waterfront homes that certainly had to run into the two-million-and-above cost bracket. Not a bad place to call home!

We saw an inviting stop just before the Palm Valley Bridge, six nautical miles after the J. Turner Butler Boulevard Bridge. The Palm Valley Outdoors Bar & Grill had a tasty-looking menu and colorful blue and orange umbrellas, but it was too early in our day for lunch. The Palm Valley Bridge was our third fixed, sixty-five-foot bridge in that travel segment. At mile marker 758.8, it took us under State Road 210. Once we passed this bridge, we entered the Tolomato River, traveling toward St. Augustine, Florida.

At that point, all along our port side lay the Guana Tolomato Matanzas National Estuarine Research Reserve. The area from Ponte Vedra to Palm Coast encompasses seventy-six thousand acres and hosts research laboratories, classrooms, and exhibits for visitors from around the world. This non-profit enterprise protects various plants and animals through a collaboration with the Florida Department of Environmental Protection and the National Oceanic and Atmospheric Administration. It investigates issues concerning water quality, weather, marsh vegetation, and most interestingly, the benefits of oysters. Oysters are more than a delicious meal. They act as filters and remove large quantities of suspended particles of carbon while increasing the penetration of light that benefits the submerged vegetation and improves the waters. The organization builds reefs from oyster shells gathered from local restaurants, which helps prevent shoreline erosion! Who would have thought? You can learn something new every day! It is rewarding to see how the states along the ICW work to protect the land and benefit the quality of their waters.

The Tolomato River had very similar qualities, much like those on which we had just traveled. Our view from the boat showed the buildings and vegetation inhabiting both sides of the river. This growth provides protection and allows the river to maintain a sense of tranquility, which we enjoyed as we glided down its shores. Moreover, this protection allows boats to find shelter in bad weather when the ocean becomes unruly, uncomfortable, and dangerous.

From the Palm Valley Road Bridge, we traveled about 4.5 nautical miles and approached Pine Island, also part of the Guana Tolomato Matanzas National Estuarine Research Reserve. Although the loop around it is called the Tolomato River, we continued straight southward on the ICW and avoided taking the loop. After passing the lower tip of Pine Island, we traveled approximately nine nautical miles. We reached the Francis and Mary Usina Bridge, which connects St. Augustine and Vilano Beach, just before the St. Augustine Inlet. We slipped under this sixty-five-foot-tall bridge at mile marker 775.8 and headed toward our starboard side to avoid the inlet, which can spell possible trouble to those unfamiliar with it. All though it was not stormy that day, we felt it best to take no chances with the unknown.

If you have never visited St. Augustine, put it on your bucket list! That is what Captain Mike and Andrew decided to do. They chose to stay in St. Augustine and take in the sights. We continued the trip without them from that point.

Having previously visited St. Augustine, I'm familiar with its mix of European charm and Southern hospitality. It abounds with history, as one can see when touring its old historic buildings and quaint houses. Horse-drawn carriages, a city trolley, or even golf car tours can provide an easy day's transportation to see the sights. Tour guides tell tales of the past and regale travelers with ghost stories, delivering a taste of Southern history from our country's earliest era. Those tasty gourmet restaurant meals make me hungry just thinking about them!

Approaching the city of St. Augustine, we saw the stunningly beautiful Bridge of Lions, a double-leaf bascule bridge—also known as a drawbridge—connecting St. Augustine to Anastasia Island via the A1A. At only seventy-nine feet wide and eighteen feet tall, we had to stop and wait at least thirty minutes for it to open. Built during Florida's 1920-era boom years, it is a national landmark. An inductee into the National Register of Historic Places, it is recognized as one of the most beautiful bridges in the Southeastern United States. The bridge gets its name from the original two Carrara marble Medici lions sitting in the Loggia dei Lanzi in Florence, Italy. Dr. Andrew Anderson commissioned and gifted them to St. Augustine. They sit in grandeur, guarding the west end of the bridge, and are named Fiel and Firme—Faith and Firm. After renovating the bridge, the city added two more identical lions known as Pax and Peli—Peace and Happiness—to the eastern end in 2015.

If you visit this little gem of a city, remember to walk across one of the most beautiful bridges in the United States; it is a must-see. It commands you to take the nearly one-mile walk across its walkway to enjoy its lions, the beginning and end of the bridge, and the beautiful scenery as you look out from its center. Whether on land or in your boat, get your camera out for pictures because, at dawn, you can capture the beauty of the seventh-century national monument, the Castillo de San Marcos fort, or at sunset, snap the millions of lights bouncing off the Matanzas River.

If you are a history buff, this place is a must. Traveling to the southern part of the peninsula, you will enter the St. Augustine's Historic District. You will see some of the most wondrous sights, including the aforementioned Castillo de San Marcos fort, constructed from Florida's coquina rock made up of millions of seashells cemented together, creating a unique construction material. The Cathedral Basilica, the oldest Catholic Parish in the United States, resides here. Also contained within the city is the Governor's House, which housed the governors of Spain, Great Britain, and then Spain again in colonial times. The Oldest Wooden School House, constructed over two hundred years ago, is the oldest schoolhouse in the United States. It was occupied in the 1600s and gave you a real sense of living during those times. The famous Plaza de la Constitucion, where a monument stands to honor the Spanish Constitution of 1812, is also a beautiful historical sight.

Venture further into the Lincolnville section and visit the St.

Augustine Distillery, where they produce bourbon, rum, gin, and vodka—Cheers! This distillery has the pleasure of being appointed the most visited distillery in all of America. Beyond being noted for its distillery, Lincolnville played a significant role in the Civil Rights Movement of the 1960s. Here, Martin Luther King Jr. held a peaceful demonstration with protestors from the New England states. King and his companions were arrested while marching toward the Plaza de la Constitucion, a demonstration that significantly influenced the passing of the Civil Rights Act of 1964. Today, you can see the path these men walked by, noting the brass footprints in the sidewalks to signify this important event.

Last but not least, you must venture to the site of Ponce de Leone's Fountain of Youth, the Spring of Eternal Hope. No one has chased away old age by drinking the water, but it is reminiscent of our childhood learnings in history class from our old school days. The town of St. Augustine is a treasure of both Southern hospitality and national historic value—a sure winner of a place to visit. After passing under the bridge, the waterway's name changes from the Tolomato River to the Matanzas River.

Let's continue! The weather was good that day and the

Intracoastal fairly calm, although reports of the ocean indicated rougher waters. So, we planned to continue on the ICW. After passing the Bridge of Lions, we traveled down the Matanzas River for a nautical mile and a half before passing under the State Road 312 Bridge, another sixty-five-foot-tall fixed beauty, at mile marker 780.3.

Further down on our starboard side, we passed the community of St. Augustine Shores, a 2,020-acre community of thirty-five hundred homes, only minutes from the City of St. Augustine, right along the Intracoastal. The homes at various price points, range of activities, and open spaces offered there can satisfy the needs of anyone from first-time homebuyers to seniors wishing to downsize. It is an excellent place to retire or make your snowbird escape!

Cruising approximately seven miles south, we came to the Crescent Beach Bridge, which took us under State Road 206. When approaching this bascule bridge, you can signal with two toots on your horn, one long and one short, to request clearance. You can also use VHF channel 9, which we did!

Approximately three nautical miles past the Crescent Beach Bridge, Rattlesnake Island appears. Its eastern side is home to Spanish Fort Matanzas. It was built in 1740 to protect the city of St. Augustine from those whose strategy was to enter through the Matanzas Inlet, located less than one nautical mile to the island's south. If you wish to tour the fort, you should bear east to your portside, where you can dock your boat and take the ferry, the only way to access the fort.

The river here is still called the Matanzas River but quickly changes to the Summer Haven River once past the Matanzas Inlet. You can follow the Summer Haven River south, and it will ultimately return to the Matanzas River/ICW. Bearing to the starboard side will keep you away from the Matanzas Inlet.

Approximately 10.5 nautical miles down the Matanzas River, we approached the Palm Coast on our starboard side. This coastal area includes Flagler Beach, Deltona, Daytona, and Ormond Beach. Back in the 1950s, the Palm Coast was a swamp and pine forest with few inhabitants and a lone turpentine distillery, all concentrated near the local state road. The late 1960s saw the International Telephone and Telegraph (ITT) Company become a multi-national corporation worth over seven billion dollars. At ITT/Levitt & Sons, Dr. Norman Young had a different vision of the swamp and pine forest land. Dr. Young saw homes, golf courses, and recreational facilities that would entice northerners living in the cold to relocate to his Floridian dreamland, and ITT supported his vision. ITT purchased sixty-eight thousand acres and began an enormous project to build forty-eight thousand home sites, developing the largest planned community in Florida. After ITT left, the people worked to sustain and support that community. The beaches looked beautiful, manicured, and clean. Traveling down the ICW, you can glimpse the community's homes, resorts, and marinas. Dr. Young's dream certainly came true!

We approached the Hammock Dunes Bridge two nautical miles further, at mile marker 803.0. It was easy to travel through this fixed bridge's sixty-five-foot vertical opening. Up to this point, the names of the rivers are easy to follow on a map, but the next section can get confusing, depending on what navigational tools or maps you use. For that reason, I always used more than one during my pre-planning and then would rely on the boat's navigation system as we went along.

After the Hammock Dunes bridge, we traveled southward on the Matanzas River for approximately one nautical mile and saw Island Estates to our port side. Island Estates, an exclusive enclave of multi-million-dollar custom-designed homes, is controlled by a protective covenant specifying conditions and restrictions to maintain their park-like setting. These estates provide easy access to the ICW, allowing you to dock in your backyard. Visions of those homes proved difficult to see through the thick foliage guarding the coastline, so we could only imagine what they looked like. This community encompassed about the next two nautical miles.

From the tip of Island Estates, we traveled for approximately another nautical mile and a half on the Matanzas River, and depending on what navigational map we looked at, it also became known as Smith Creek. Approximate 1.8 nautical miles further down the Smith Creek, we came to the Flagler/Moody Boulevard Bridge.

We cruised southward under the fixed Flagler/Moody Boulevard Bridge, opening at mile marker 810.6, with a sixty-five-foot vertical opening, with no problems. The two names of this waterway, the Matanzas River or Smith Creek, continued for the next 2.4 nautical miles. It then changed to Halifax Creek but again had a second name, distinguishing it as the Matanzas River. I have never encountered such a variety of names in the North, but Southerners like a wide variety. However, the most important thing to remember is that it is all the Intracoastal Waterway or the ICW!

Roughly 2.2 nautical miles south, on the ICW/Matanzas/Smith Creek, wouldn't you know it—the name changed again! The ICW was now being called Halifax Creek. We traveled on Halifax Creek for 2.4 nautical miles and approached a bascule bridge named the L. B. Knox/Highbridge Road Bridge, at mile marker 816.0. It is another bascule bridge that opens on a signal with a one-two toot or by calling on VHF channel 9.

Just after the L.B. Knox/Highbridge Road Bridge, guess what? Yep, another river name change! It is either called Halifax Creek or Halifax River. We traveled 2.2 nautical miles on Halifax Creek. Then, when it became Halifax River, we continued another approximately 5.6 nautical miles to the W. Granada Boulevard/Ormond Beach Bridge at mile marker 824.9. This fixed, sixty-five-foot vertical footbridge was another easy one to go under, and on we continued.

The next area of the ICW, past Ormond Beach, continued to be called the Halifax River. We were approaching five bridges leading to the Daytona Beach area, all very near each other. The first was Seabreeze/Oakridge Twin Bridges, at mile marker 824.9. It had a sixty-five-foot vertical clearance. Approximately half a nautical mile further, the second was Main Street Bridge, at mile marker 829.7, another fixed sixty-five-foot clearance we quickly traveled through. The third was the famous International Speedway Boulevard Bridge that leads directly into Daytona International Speedway.

As a quick side note, if you ever want to take a break from boating and enjoy motorcycles as much as I do, then you really need to do Daytona Bike Week at least once in your life! March 2023 saw the eighty-second anniversary of Daytona Bike Week. Events include festival activities, swamp meets, the famous path called The Loop, and many other motorcycle-enthusiast attractions.

If you're not into bumping your butt along on a motorcycle, the famous Daytona 500 NASCAR race is in February and you can dock your boat and easily get to the raceway for this fabulous event. Before 1953, cars raced on the hard-packed sand of Daytona Beach. The year 1954 saw Mr. Bill France Sr. contract with the City of Daytona to build this speedway, and in 1959, a crowd of forty-one thousand saw the first race. After a 2013 renovation, it now seats 101,500. This is the big one we all watch on television! Zoom, zoom, zoom!

As a sideline, if you're into older vintage cars beach racing, take your boat to a dock near Wildwood, New Jersey, for a unique look at a race called The Race of Gentlemen (TROG) in early October. The first Race of the Gentlemen occurred in 1905 on the New Jersey beach of Cape May. It saw the likes of Henry Ford, Louis Chevrolet, and speed-holder John Walter Christie, an engineering genius who was the first to incorporate the idea of front-wheel drive. The year 2008 saw Mel Stutz and the ten members of The Oilers Car Club, a motorcycle club founded in 1947, recreate The Race of Gentlemen on the beach in Asbury Park, New Jersey. Later, due to the effects of Hurricane Sandy, it moved to Wildwood, New Jersey, the world's du-wop capital, a town entrenched in 1960s-era style. This race features pre-WWII automobiles and motorcycles that race from 8 a.m. to sunset on the beach, with a big bonfire party with food and music to celebrate the end! The race also has a West Coast version in Riverside, California, with another version that takes place in the United Kingdom.

But enough of that—back to the *Sea Scape*'s adventure in Florida. The fourth bridge in this immediate beach area, the lovely Memorial Bridge, is a mere half-nautical-mile further south, at mile marker 830.6; we flowed under its sixty-five-foot vertical clearance, then, almost five nautical miles further on the Halifax River, we came to the fifth bridge. The A1A Port Orange Relief Bridge, at mile marker 835.5, was another easy run as we traveled beneath its sixty-five-foot vertical clearance.

Once past the A1A Port Orange Relief Bridge, we wanted to avoid the Ponce de Leon Inlet. It can be tricky and dangerous, with continuously changing shoals, where buoy markings can change rapidly. I know enough boats that have gone aground in this inlet. Therefore, I wanted to avoid that area, especially considering the *Sea Scape*'s five-foot draft. I wasn't taking any chances. So, we followed the Halifax River south for 3.7 nautical miles until we came to Piddler Island. We then followed the island's shore, on our starboard side, for about three nautical miles, heading for the Ponce de Leon Cut and then reaching back to the ICW, which at that point went by the name of the Indian River or Indian River North.

Roughly 5.8 nautical miles further, we reached the George E. Mussen/Coronado Beach Bridge, which took us under Florida State Road 44. At mile marker 845.0, this bascule bridge opens on a signal—except between the hours of 7 a.m. to 7 p.m.—every half-hour on the hour, seven days a week. Our luck was with us, and as we slowly approached the bridge, it opened as if on cue.

Once past the George E. Musson/Coronado Beach Bridge, we headed five nautical miles south around Chicken Island. I cannot tell you why, but just its name made my mouth water! I guess I was getting hungry! We then came to the Harris Saxon South Causeway

Bridge. This fixed sixty-five-footer, at mile marker 846.5, told me we were getting closer to our destination!

As we cruised down the Indian River North for the next 17.8 nautical miles, the Mosquito Lagoon appeared toward our port side. This 111-square-mile brackish water lagoon is part of the Indian River Lagoon system, an Estuary of National Significance. It can be very shallow in many parts with a depth of only three to four feet, not a place for the *Sea Scape*. It claims to have the best redfish in the world. Redfish, which some might recognize as red snapper, is a game fish with a mild, sweet, firm consistency suitable for grilling, baking, or frying—and I'm getting hungry all over again!

As we came near the end of the Indian River North/Mosquito Lagoon, we had to turn westward and enter the Haulover Canal that cuts through Merritt Island, connecting the Indian River Lagoon and Mosquito Lagoon. Dug out initially by enslaved people of a local citrus grower, shoals accumulated and made it inadequate. It was named after the practice of hauling larger boats over rollers. It had been abandoned for a time, but when the Intracoastal Waterway was designed, the Army Corps of Engineers crafted a deeper canal with a draw bridge connecting the two sides of Merritt Island. NASA propelled the area into the twentieth century by replacing the draw bridge with a taller, double-leaf, bascule two-lane bridge named the Allenhurst (Haulover Canal) Bridge. It stands at mile marker 869.2 and opens by request via VHF channel 9. We went slow and saw a beautiful show of West Indian manatees as we slid across the canal! Above the bridge is an observation deck to watch those manatees put on their show. A delight to see!

Once out of the canal, we crossed under three more bridges before our turn toward the Bluepoints Marina, our destination for the day. We continued westward for nearly 2.5 nautical miles on the body of water, now only called the Indian River, not the Indian River North. After about four nautical miles, we turned southward to our first bridge, the NASA (Jay-Jay) Railroad Bridge. This bascule bridge, at marker 876.6, is usually open unless a train is coming. So, with none in view, we had an easy pass as we got nearer our destination for the day.

Just about two nautical miles further, at mile marker 878.9, we came to the second bridge in that section of our journey. The A. Max Brewer Bridge allowed us to pass under State Road 406, one of the roads you can take into Cape Canaveral. Mile marker 885.0 gave us our third bridge, the NASA Causeway Bridge, about six nautical miles south. Also listed as the John F. Kennedy Space Center Bridge, it took us under State Road 405, which leads drivers directly into Cape Canaveral.

Just before we approached the Bennett Causeway Bridge, we turned east onto the Canaveral Barge Canal and traveled 2.9 nautical miles across Merritt Island. We entered a body of water called the Banana River for a mere nautical mile. Next, we entered the Canaveral Lock.

Going through this lock is quite an adventure. Using our VHF channel 13, we announced our intent to use the lock and our position to the lock master, who communicated a clear set of directions with army precision. First and foremost, he insisted that everybody wear their floatation device before entering the lock. He told us that once he was sure the channel was cleared, he would signal us to proceed by either a blinking green traffic light at the top left of the lock door or through the VHF channel—or by using both. He then told us to have our mooring lines ready so we could secure the boat once in the lock; once inside the lock, we were to remain tied up until we were given the signal to proceed. He reminded us that the lock was a no-wake and no-fishing zone, and it was in the best interest of all those using the lock for us to move as far down as possible to allow room for others inside the lock. We prepared our lines and began to pay attention to the traffic light signal.

Approximately thirty minutes later, we moved the boat into the lock. Two heavy concrete, steel, and wooden doors opened on both sides, allowing the *Sea Scape* to enter the lock. At the opening, the red light changed to blinking green, the signal to allow our boat to advance through the doors, and the lock master told us it was okay to move forward. Since we were the only boat going through the lock at that time, we could tie it to either side of the lock once we entered it. No assistant arrived to help us with anything in the lock once we entered, so we immediately went to work. We needed to tie the lines onto pilings with insufficient cleats on the bulkhead. If we failed to secure the boat properly, it could have broken free and caused damage to itself, the lock doors, or even other boats in the lock if any had been present. Those lines would hold the boat in place while the water moved in and out, causing a current within the lock. Additionally, we had to be careful to ensure the boat did not get stuck on the rails on the lock wall. Getting stuck on the walls could cause the boat to capitulate and turn sideward into the water—a total disaster!

We watched the water level slowly change in the lock, increasing about eighteen inches, which we later learned was about the average amount of change. The entire process took about thirty minutes. We enjoyed an amazing show of nature in between watching the sides of the boat to ensure they wouldn't get stuck on the lock rails! Like a sentinel of guards lining the edge of the lock, we saw hundreds of pelicans. They appeared to segregate, with the white pelicans in one group and the gray pelicans in another. I had never seen white pelicans and did not know much about them, but I watched in amazement as they dove into the water, hunting for food. We had another surprise when we saw dolphins swimming and jumping along the side of the boat and then were joined by the roly-poly manatees inside the lock waters. It was as if the lock had become a playpen for them all. A spectacle beyond imagination! We could have stayed there for much longer watching the show Mother Nature put on, but our time inside this lock was over. After being given the signal, we unhitched our lines and exited the lock. That experience was undoubtedly memorable.

As we exited, a few hundred yards past the lock, we saw the SR 401 Bridge. We called the bridge tender on VHF channel 9, and shortly, he opened this bascule bridge, and we cruised on through. Less than one nautical mile further, we arrived at Bluepoints Marina, our destination for that day.

Port Canaveral is huge, accommodating many cruise ships and a variety of personal boating vessels.

Bluepoints Marina, the newest state-of-the-art marina in the area, was our choice for the night. It was reasonably priced and catered to a high number of steady fishermen. That marina is serious about taking care of your boat and has the foresight to protect it during any fierce, raging hurricane weather in its fully enclosed, dry storage facility, which has a wind load rating of 150 mph for hurricane protection. In addition, it offers hurricane protection plans and has deep water and well-marked approaches. Concierge service is available; if you wish, your boat can be ready at the courtesy docks fully loaded with bait, beverages, snacks, deli food, and any additional supplies offered by its ship store. Fishermen surely love their twenty-four-hour extensive fish cleaning and boat washing stations. I found the trophy board, which allows fishermen/women to display pictures of their catch, incredibly unique. We fishing people always like to share our prize catch! Since they do not cater to transient vessels, we were lucky to get a slip for the *Sea Scape*— especially after finding out what the night would entail!

It was around five in the evening when we docked. We tied our lines and connected our electricity to wash up and get ready to chow down because we were hungry! As we took care of docking

duties, I noticed that the marina appeared extremely busy, more so than most marinas at that time of day. After striking up a conversation with someone at the dock, I found out that we had picked the right night to dock there since a great spectacle was forthcoming! That night, the *Orion* spacecraft from the Artemis program was going into outer space. The marina at Port Canaveral was only a few miles from the launch site at the Kennedy Space Center, a perfect site for watching this exhibition. People had come from all over to watch the takeoff from their boats, scheduled for two in the morning. We were very excited to witness such a magnificent historical event, which we had only learned about after arriving at that marina. Talk about fortunate! Due to bad weather and mechanical issues, the event had been canceled multiple times before that night.

Since no restaurants were close enough to walk our tired bodies

to, we decided to eat on the *Sea Scape* and worked up a quick meal of pasta and meat sauce with a big salad. Knowing that a full night's sleep wouldn't be possible, given the circumstances, we only sat and relaxed together for a short time. We were tired from the day's voyage and figured we could get some shut-eye before the takeoff. Setting our alarms to wake up before two in the morning, we jumped in our beds and took a long snooze!

Red-eyed and bushy-tailed, we woke up before 2 a.m. and headed to the bow of the *Sea Scape*. We were fortunate to be blessed with a clear night sky. With our binoculars ready, we turned on our cellular phones and listened as CNN described the event, attempting to capture the moment with our own eyes.

As we sat on the bow, we witnessed a massive glowing ball of fire leave the ground. Rolling and pivoting our necks like cranes while watching the sky, we almost fell backward to follow the enormous glow. Though too far away to hear the thunderous sound of the takeoff, it still felt like we were right there on the tarmac, watching the vessel go up into the black but flawless night sky. We watched the fireball and, within a few minutes, saw the separation of the rocket before it disappeared into the night sky.

It was an unbelievable sight, mesmerizing us for several seconds. Still, we quickly refocused and took videos and photos with our cell phones, getting great shots. We were even able to capture the separation of the rocket. Being there that night was a magnificent stroke of luck. I had never seen a rocket go into space, so the opportunity proved enormously exciting.

The entire launch event took less than an hour. It was not easy to go directly to sleep after seeing what occurred. I was pumped up and excited, with an incredible need to share my exhilaration.

Sometime after 3 a.m., I began texting videos and pictures to my friends and family. I know they thought I was crazy, but you would have done the same if you were there. By then, I was exhausted and ready to get some sleep because tomorrow would be another busy day, heading to our final destination. The next day, when I awoke, I had to ask myself if what I saw had been real. It almost resembled a dream or something seen on television, but I had the proof in my photos that what I witnessed was real. It was such an unforgettable experience!

The following day, we had a slow, groggy start from our interrupted sleep, but a couple of cups of coffee did the trick, and we came alive and started on our way. That night, we discussed reporting by CNN, coming to the consensus that there should have been more connection between the visual experience of the sendoff and CNN's description of the event. CNN's description was always a few seconds behind what we saw. It was like getting the video feedback of a play at a football game rather than seeing it in real time. All day, we continued to bring the conversation back to the launch, noting details that had particularly thrilled us and discussing how, like many other significant historical events, none of us would ever forget that one. It will remain locked in my memory bank forever. Seeing that pink sky that morning was indeed a lucky sign!

OVERVIEW

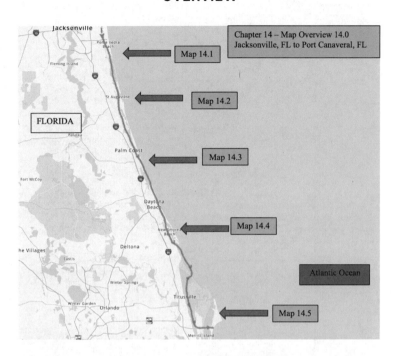

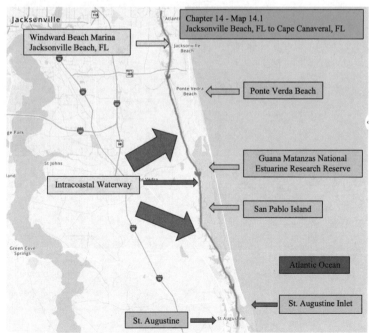

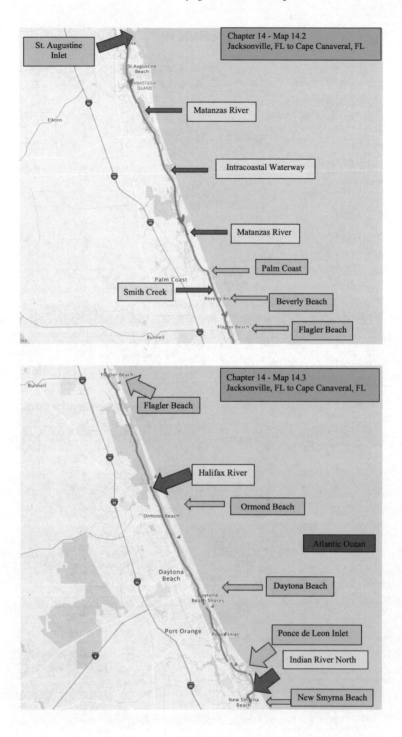

Chapter 14 - Map 14.2
Jacksonville, FL to Cape Canaveral, FL

St. Augustine Inlet

Matanzas River

Intracoastal Waterway

Matanzas River

Palm Coast

Smith Creek

Beverly Beach

Flagler Beach

Chapter 14 - Map 14.3
Jacksonville, FL to Cape Canaveral, FL

Flagler Beach

Halifax River

Ormond Beach

Atlantic Ocean

Daytona Beach

Ponce de Leon Inlet

Indian River North

New Smyrna Beach

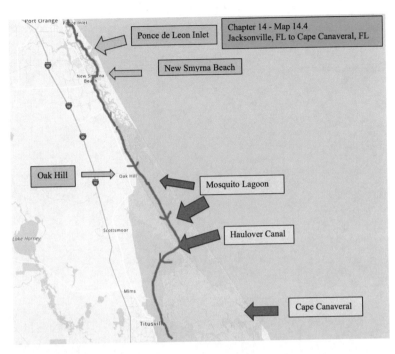

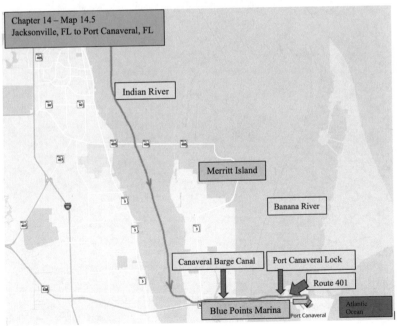

ALMOST HOME!

"There comes a time in every rightly constructed boy's life when he has a raging desire to go somewhere and dig for hidden treasure"

—Mark Twain

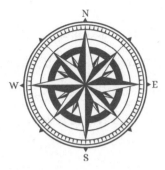

November 17, 2022

Blue Point Marina
Port Canaveral, Florida
To
Fort Pierce, City Marina
Fort Pierce, Florida

We dawned on the thirteenth day since beginning our voyage from New Jersey. The weather was good, with blue skies and a few wispy clouds in the atmosphere. There was no chance of rain, but the ocean was still churning out wave heights of five to eight feet, so we decided to stay on the Intracoastal and head to Fort Pierce, Florida, our next stop.

Being people of habit, my first mate and I woke early that morning and had our usual coffee and conversations about the day and route to come. Though slightly fatigued, I knew that given an hour or so to shake the sleepiness from my head, I would be fine. Some food and coffee also helped do the trick.

We untied our lines, disconnected the electricity, measured the engine oil, and prepared to leave the dock. We left the dock at around 8 a.m., came out of Bluepoints Marina in Port Canaveral, and headed west to make our trip in reverse and then head south on the Indian River.

Approximately half a nautical mile west of Bluepoints Marina, we reached the SR 401 Bridge. We called the bridge tender, a delightful woman, on VHF channel 9 and requested that she open the bridge. I find it interesting to see a woman bridge tender, not a job many women would undertake, but why not! Our wait was only about ten minutes, and we then moved under the bridge and continued west to enter the Canaveral Lock, the largest lock in Florida.

The Canaveral Lock's purpose is to reduce the tidal-current velocities and hurricane tides in the Canaveral harbor, a very big harbor for ocean liners. The lock allows for the safe passage of vessels from the Banana River to Port Canaveral and onto the Atlantic Ocean. Preventing flooding and accidents during heavy rainfall requires reducing the speed and flow of water. Built bigger than initially planned, it also accommodated the *Saturn* rocket's first stage. Can you imagine seeing part of a rocket coming through the lock! It must have been an incredible sight! Any boat with a draft of less than twelve feet can enter the lock for passage. I wonder how big the boat carrying the rocket's first stage must have been!

We planned to go through the lock again, only this time heading west. Then we would cross west over the Banana River and then continue west through the Canaveral Barge Canal. That plan would lead us to the Indian River. We traveled west on the Indian River for 0.8 nautical miles, then turned south for 0.1 nautical miles, and finally headed under the Bennett Memorial Bridge at mile marker 894.0. That twin-span fixed bridge offers a sixty-five-foot vertical clearance and a ninety-foot horizontal opening, so we had no problems.

As we continued down the Indian River, along the coast of Merritt Island for another 2.6 nautical miles, we approached the Hubert Humphrey Bridge at mile marker 897.4, another twin-span fixed bridge with a sixty-five-foot vertical clearance.

Approximately 9.4 nautical miles south, as we cruised along the long, whittled tip of Merritt Island, we approached the fixed Pineda Causeway Bridge at mile marker 909.0. Our navigation system told us to travel carefully because the reader boards were slightly off, but we had no problems. This bridge leads you to Merritt Island's Patrick Air Force Base, which supports our United States Space Force at NASA's Kennedy Space Center, located on Merritt Island.

A mere 4.5 nautical miles south, we glided under the fixed Eau Gallie Causeway Bridge. Located at mile marker 914.4, this sixty-five-foot vertical clearance bridge leads to the community of Indian Harbour Beach on Cape Canaveral. Area Vibes, a data analytics and real estate company, rates Indian Harbor Beach, along with Palm Beach and Sanibel Island, as the top three Florida communities in which to live. I have never been to Indian Harbour Beach but have visited Palm Beach and Sanibel Island. What can I say about Palm Beach, located on Florida's east coast? Well, what comes to mind is old-school opulence, sophistication, elegance, and a myriad of social events. Sanibel Island, on Florida's west coast offers beautiful sunsets, white sand, blue water, dolphins, and luxury accommodations; most importantly, it is the seashell capital of the world. As you walk along the beach you can't help but develop the "Sanibel Stoop" as you constantly bend over to pick up another seashell, with each one more beautiful than the last! Definitely another place for your bucket list!

On this marvelous day, we continued south a short 3.0 nautical miles and cruised through Melbourne. We crossed under the Melbourne Causeway Bridge, another twin-span fixed bridge leading to the Canaveral National Seashore, at mile marker 918.2, with no glitches.

The Indian River remained wide and deep for the next twenty-four miles, and then, just after we passed under the fixed Wabasso Bridge, at mile marker 943.3, we approached Indian River Shores. The area between Florida's Space Coast and Gold Coast is called the Treasure Coast and includes Sebastian, Vero Beach, Port St. Lucie, Hobe Sound, Jupiter, and our destination, Fort Pierce. It was so named in 1961 after salvagers recovered some of the treasure from a Spanish Treasure Fleet sunk during a 1715 hurricane. Visitors to their beaches can occasionally find a piece of gold or silver from the treasure still lying on the bottom of the ocean floor when it washes up to the shoreline. This area of the Indian River Lagoon boasts some stunning, upscale multi-million-dollar homes, many of which peeked out to us as we traveled down the ICW.

At this point, the ICW becomes narrower but still easy to navigate. We approached the fixed Merrill P. Barber Bridge at mile marker 951.9, some 3.7 nautical miles south of Sebastian, the first city of the Treasure Coast. We did not encounter any hassles crossing under this bridge. Then, a scant nautical mile further, we moved smoothly under the fixed Alma Lee Loy Bridge, mile marker 953.2, a sixty-five-foot vertical bridge.

Some 9.5 nautical miles south, on the Indian River, we approached our first bascule bridge, the D.H. Banty Saunders Bridge, also known as the SR A1A, North Causeway Bridge. By 2027, an eight-five-foot vertical fixed bridge will replace this bascule bridge. The bascule was open, so there was no wait, but the Fort Pierce Inlet stood between this bridge and the fixed Peter B. Cobb Memorial Bridge, which was only half a nautical mile further. We maneuvered past the Fort Pierce Inlet, which could be strong and turbulent, but we knew it well and were attentive to its markings and the buoys at its entrance. Skillfully, we crossed it and flowed under the next bridge, the Peter B. Cobb Memorial Bridge.

The city of Fort Pierce, noted as a quaint fishing village of the past, now offers the types of modern accouterments we all enjoy. The Fort Pierce City Marina, only three-tenths of a nautical mile away and located along the Treasure Coast, is newly renovated, beautiful, state-of-the-art, publicly owned, and has slips for forty transient boats. Those renovations took into consideration the space needed for catamarans like the *Sea Scape*, and it had a slip that easily accommodated my yacht.

The amenities at the marina include Wi-Fi, a pump out, showers, a fish cleaning station, two fuel stations, 30/50/100-amp service, a laundry, and ice. It is also within walking distance of shops, restaurants, theaters, and museums. Not wanting to cook, two dockside restaurants offered us plenty of dining choices for the night. We chose Crabby's Dockside and, after going back and forth, finally settled on pizza since we hadn't savored that dish in a while. According to *Food & Wine* magazine, our home state of New Jersey has the best pizza in the United States, so we went for the next best thing: The New Yorker Pizza. What else? It was a mouth-watering hand-thrown classic, topped with pepperoni and Italian sausage that would have made my local Jersey pizza maker proud. It was, in fact, a close match to our New Jersey pizza! The perfect choice!

Afterward, we took a short stroll, but since we were tired, we returned to the *Sea Scape*, calling it an early night. Only one more leg of our journey, and we would be at our homes in Fort Lauderdale. We wanted an early start, so we said goodnight and sweet dreams.

OVERVIEW

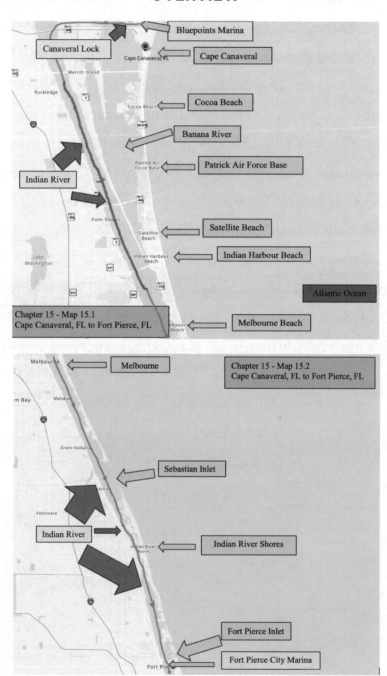

Bluepoints Marina

Canaveral Lock

Cape Canaveral

Cocoa Beach

Banana River

Patrick Air Force Base

Indian River

Satellite Beach

Indian Harbour Beach

Atlantic Ocean

Chapter 15 - Map 15.1
Cape Canaveral, FL to Fort Pierce, FL

Melbourne Beach

Melbourne

Chapter 15 - Map 15.2
Cape Canaveral, FL to Fort Pierce, FL

Sebastian Inlet

Indian River

Indian River Shores

Fort Pierce Inlet

Fort Pierce City Marina

HOME - SWEET - HOME

" It is good to have an end to journey toward;
but it is the journey that matters, in the end."

—Ernest Hemingway

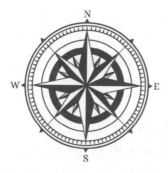

November 18, 2022

Fort Pierce City Marina
Fort Pierce, Florida
To
Home
Fort Lauderdale, Florida

It may have been the anticipation of getting home, but I awoke just as the sun was starting to rise. Lauri made us a quick breakfast—some coffee and cereal, and we were on our way. After leaving the beautiful Fort Pierce City Marina, we were excited about how close we were to home. As we traveled the 17.0 nautical miles, the ICW was about one nautical mile wide and easy to navigate. Passing Port St. Lucie, we approached the Jensen Beach Causeway Bridge, the Frank A. Wacha/State Road 707-A Bridge. This fixed, sixty-five-foot, vertical clearance bridge stood at mile marker 981.4, and as was the case with nearly 99 percent of all sixty-five-foot bridges I've encountered, it was an easy go. Three nautical miles further, we approached another fixed bridge at mile marker 984.9, the Ernest Lyons Bridge/SR A1A, with the town of Stuart coming just after this bridge. This bridge, thanks to its fixed sixty-five-foot clearance, presented no problems.

Roughly 2.5 nautical miles further along the ICW, at the confluence of the Indian River, the St. Lucie River, the Okeechobee Waterway, and the ICW, we passed what is known as The Crossroads or the Saint Lucie Inlet. The inlet has a reputation for being a tough go. Sport fishermen and mega yachts mainly use it. This inlet is under continuous monitoring due to shoaling and strong currents. Night-time navigation is highly discouraged. As we passed The Crossroads/Saint Lucie Inlet, we entered the ICW, with Jupiter Island to our port side. The small body of water we traveled on was Peck Lake, also part of the ICW.

St. Lucie Inlet Preserve State Park, part of Jupiter Island, was on our port side as we traveled down the much narrower ICW. The park boasts almost three miles of white sandy beach for sunbathers to enjoy and is home to leatherback, green, and loggerhead turtles, so watch out for the babies! The Anastasia Rock Reef rests off its shore, with stunning examples of Florida coral and tropical fish. Docks are provided there that are perfect for just sitting and fishing. Its slogan says it all: "Take nothing with you but photos and leave nothing behind but ripples!"

All along the ICW on this leg of our journey, the local name of the ICW frequently changed as we traveled a little south. Here, the ICW is now called South Jupiter Narrows. As we cruised the 6.7 nautical miles southward to Hobe Sound, a town and a sound, we approached the Hobe Sound Bridge, a bascule bridge at mile marker 995.9, which opens with a ninety-foot clearance. It was an easy passage after alerting the bridge tender on VHF channel 9.

We traveled the ICW here, better known as Hobe Sound, which widens again for some 3.7 nautical miles. It then narrows again for approximately 3.5 nautical miles and is, at that point, called Jupiter Sound. We then approached the Jupiter Island Bridge/CR 707 at mile marker 1004.1. Our navigation system told us to hail this bridge as the 707 bridge, which we did. It was another bascule bridge and a pleasant bridge tender who easily accommodated us. He allowed for a cooperative, calm passage.

We now approached Jupiter, which some say is part of the Treasure Coast, while others insist it is part of the Gold Coast. The Gold Coast area houses a high population of residents from northeastern states such as Massachusetts, Connecticut, New York, and New Jersey. Many notable celebrities live in the Jupiter area such as Tiger Woods, Celine Dion, Greg Norman, Michael Jordan, and the late Burt Reynolds, Jupiter's favorite son, to name but a few.

With approximately fifty-three nautical miles left to travel, we had to pass through twenty-seven additional bridges—about one bridge per two nautical miles! Ugh! All except one were bascule-type bridges. I often wonder why they did not just erect fixed bridges, which, though they have a higher initial cost to construct, are more cost-efficient with their unchanging shapes and positions. Once erected, they are permanent fixtures that, unlike a bascule bridge, require little maintenance nor bridge tenders to operate them.

Additionally, for the boat owner, they cause no bottleneck of vessels passing under them. For automobile drivers, they have less chance of malfunctioning and getting stuck in the up position. But many of these bridges, though old, are still very serviceable. Other than the low construction costs, I can think of no other reason why those bascule-type replacement bridges continue to be erected!

The following section had a few twists and turns. Immediately after the Jupiter Island Bridge, we encountered the waters of the Jupiter Inlet—a passage so unsafe that it is not even considered passable when the ocean produces any swells. My best advice is to stay away from its turbulent waters altogether.

We traveled a scant 0.3 nautical miles south, then made a sharp turn starboard and traveled another 0.3 nautical miles under the bascule U.S. 1 Jupiter Bridge/Jupiter Federal Bridge (the first of twenty-seven, mind you). When replaced, the area will see a new double-leaf drawbridge, not a fixed bridge. The bridge tender there was very accommodating, and we flew under it. Two-tenths of a nautical mile past this bridge, we made a sharp turn to the port side and headed down Lake Worth Creek on our way through Florida's Gold Coast.

A scant 0.7 nautical miles later, we approached the second bridge on our list: Indiantown Bridge. Our navigational app noted that the bascule bridge opened every thirty minutes on the hour and the half hour. Curiously, we had to wait five minutes past the hour—maybe the bridge tender's watch read differently than ours! Once past Jupiter and the Indiantown Bridge, the ICW, still known here as Lake Worth Creek, became much narrower again, but as long as we paid attention to the marked buoys, we had no problems in navigation.

We traveled 3.2 nautical miles south without incident and approached the third bridge: Donald Ross Bridge at mile marker 1009.3, Juno Beach. Another bascule bridge that opens every hour and a half hour. That bridge opened for us five minutes before the half-hour, to our delight! Thank you, Mr. Bridge Tender! Onward!

The next area of the coastline is known as the Gold Coast. Major cities along the Gold Coast area include the towns past Jupiter down to Miami, with Fort Lauderdale on the list. As mentioned, Fort Lauderdale, our final destination, is considered the boating capital of the world. Just fifty-three nautical miles to go. I had traveled this path before and anticipated the numerous bridges we would encounter. The Gold Coast's population is quite large, especially during the winter with the arrival of all the "snowbirds," those northerners coming down to escape the winter cold! The towns along the Gold Coast built many bridges to accommodate the high volume of people and cars crossing over to the beaches on the barrier island. Everyone wants to get to the beach!

We traveled only 0.7 nautical miles and were then required to turn to our starboard for a short 0.2 nautical miles and then back straight south for another 2.2 nautical miles. Since, aside from boating, golf is a way of life down there, we reached the appropriately named PGA Boulevard Bridge, which, you guessed it, was another bascule bridge! Those Floridians enjoy golf so much, they named a street and the bridge after the PGA (Professional Golfers Association). Just past the PGA Bridge, my excitement grew because we were getting even closer!

About half a nautical mile past the PGA Bridge, we turned toward our portside, and then about 0.7 nautical miles later, we approached the Parker Bridge at mile marker 1012.6 (bridge five of twenty-seven), and yes, it was another bascule bridge. Doing our homework, we learned that bridge opens on a quarter-hour and three-quarter hours schedule. Realizing we had to time our travel to meet the schedule, we slowed down considerably.

A short 0.3 nautical miles further, we entered Lake Worth at North Palm Beach. We followed that broad body of water south for 3.6 nautical miles before approaching the Blue Heron Bridge/A1A, our only fixed bridge of the twenty-seven bridges, with a vertical clearance of sixty-five feet, located at mile marker 1017.2. It was a breeze to cruise under! The Lake Worth area is abundant with condominiums and hotels, making it a paradise for snowbirds!

Once past the Blue Heron Bridge, we traveled less than a short nautical mile south, keeping Peanut Island on our starboard side to avoid the Palm Beach/Lake Worth Inlet, which was artificially made in 1880 when settlers cut through the barrier island and into the Lake Worth Lagoon. We traveled down Lake Worth for 3.9 nautical miles and approached the West Palm Beach/Flagler Memorial Bridge, a bascule bridge at mile marker 1021.8. This bridge, which sits north of the Whitehall Mansion, now the famous Flagler Museum, also lies just east of the famous Breakers Hotel, facing the Atlantic Ocean. About seven marinas can be found from Riviera Beach to Palm Beach, and a few hour's layover at one of them can afford you the opportunity to learn some outstanding history.

Henry Flagler, along with John D. Rockefeller, founded Standard Oil, once the world's largest oil refinery. Flagler was an early Florida advocate who helped create the modern Florida we know today. Once one of the poorest states in the union, Flagler saw great things for the swamp land and worked to make his dream of a Florida railroad to Key West a reality. His efforts raised Florida's economy to reflect its status today. Whether familiar with Florida's history or not, you must take the time to visit the Flagler Museum and the Breakers Hotel. There, you will learn much about Florida and Henry Flagler, one of the great United States industrialists of the Gilded Age.

Flagler's Whitehall and The Breakers Hotel stand as monuments to his ambition and, more importantly, his foresight. Whitehall's Gilded Age Mansion, today known as the Flagler Museum, is a tribute to his work. It holds a place on the list of National Historic Landmarks. The magnificence of the physical buildings and their history, along with accounts of his other accomplishments in Florida, serve as lessons of what made Henry Flagler and this country great. The museum tour is highly informative and well worth the time. His collection of antique clocks alone is worth the visit! They are fantastic to see!

A short distance away stands The Breakers Hotel, a stunning example of Renaissance Revival architecture. The Breakers was initially called the Wayside Inn, then renamed the Palm Beach Inn. Its third and last name change came in 1901 when Henry Flagler renamed it The Breakers since many guests requested rooms "over by the breakers." Two fires, with the second in 1925, saw the hotel renovated. Unfortunately, Henry Flagler died in May of 1913 and never got to see the Renaissance Revival style reflected in today's version of The Breakers. That magnificent hotel, modeled after the Villa Medici in Italy, has the most beautiful, intricate paintings, some of which span the length of its two-hundred-foot lobby ceilings. Famous guests there include the Rockefellers, the Vanderbilts, the Astors, Andrew Carnegie, J.P. Morgan, and U.S. presidents Truman, Ford, Reagan, and G.H.W. Bush. Walk the grounds and enjoy the view, step inside to see the beautiful artwork, and don't forget to grab a cocktail in their unique aquarium bar—yes, the bar is one long fish tank!

A short distance past the Flagler Memorial Bridge, not even a half a nautical mile south, was the Royal Park Bridge/SR 704 (bridge eight out of twenty-seven), another bascule, at mile marker 1022.6, opening on the hour and half-hour. We were lucky and timed both bridges to optimize their openings.

We came to the Southern Boulevard Bridge at mile marker 1024.7, only 1.7 nautical miles south, with Mar-a-Lago, the famous multi-million-dollar private club resort owned by Donald Trump, standing on the Atlantic Ocean side of this barrier island, just to the north of this bridge. The Southern Boulevard Bridge, a bascule bridge, had an outstanding bridge tender. He told us to hurry and snuck us through, even though we were a bit late for their quarter/three-quarter-hour openings.

Continuing our travels on Lake Worth, the waterway remained wide and comfortable for the *Sea Scape*, and after 3.4 nautical miles further south, we approached the Lake Avenue Bridge at mile marker 1028.8—another bascule bridge, this one opening upon signal, which made it an easy go. We then approached the town of Lantana and the Lantana Bridge/East Ocean Avenue Bridge at mile marker 1031.0 (number eleven out of twenty-seven for those of you keeping count). While at the Fort Pierce City Marina, someone told us it was best to hail this bridge as the Lantana Bridge and not the East Ocean Avenue Bridge because, 3.4 nautical miles south of there, we would find the Boynton Beach/East Ocean Avenue Bridge at mile marker 1035.0. That bridge hails as the East Ocean Avenue Bridge. So, mislabeling the bridges when hailing them can present a mountain of confusion. They are both bascule bridges with openings on the hour and half hour. You would think they would time them like they do traffic lights! Knowing this, we slowed considerably to be there at the half-hour mark and glided through. With 3.4 nautical miles to go to the Boynton Beach/East Ocean Avenue Bridge, we took our time getting there and passed through with no problem. A short 0.7 nautical miles further, we slipped under the E. Woolbright Road Bridge, which thankfully opened upon request.

After Boynton Beach, the ICW narrows and continues in this manner for about the next seven nautical miles. Almost two miles south of the E. Woolbright Road Bridge, we reached the George Bush Boulevard Bridge with the next bridge, the Atlantic Avenue Bridge, coming into view at a mere 0.7 nautical miles south, at Delray Beach. Like most areas along the Intracoastal, Delray has homes and condominiums to which northern snowbirds flock! Just a short 1.3 nautical miles later, we met the Linton Boulevard

Bridge (bridge sixteen of twenty-seven) at mile marker 1041.0, another bascule bridge opening on the hour and the half-hour with a relaxed passage. A little over three nautical miles south, we came to the Spanish River Boulevard Bridge at mile marker 1044.9, a bascule bridge that also opens on the hour and half-hour.

The waterway began to get a little wider as we entered Lake Wyman, then narrows for the next nautical mile, leaving Lake Wyman. After another short nautical mile, we approached the Palmetto Park Bridge at mile marker 1047.5. This bascule bridge has an hour, and half-hour schedule and was bustling with boating traffic. Because of its narrow opening, I was extra cautious to avoid any damage to my *Sea Scape*! We then entered Lake Boca Raton, which will lead you to the Atlantic Ocean through the Boca Inlet Bridge, but we wanted to stay on the ICW and continue bearing south, cruising through Boca Raton.

The hotels, condominiums, and homes that line the white sandy beaches of Boca Raton project a lifestyle of luxury and extravagance. This style was not by chance but rather by the design of Florida's most famous architect, Addison Mizner. The 1920s saw Mizner gather a herald list of investors, which included the likes of Paris Singer, from the Singer Sewing Machine fortune; John Wanamaker, retail department store giant; Elizabeth Arden, of the famed cosmetic empire; and Irving Berlin, American composer and lyricist, to mention a few. Using the funds provided by these investors, he worked to create his dream city, Bocaratone, which later was changed to Boca Raton. Mizner's Mediterranean Revival and Spanish Colonial Revival style is still evident today. The city then and now eludes the fantasy and romance that Mizner wanted to create. If you are interested in architecture, park your boat at one of the three marinas in this area and visit the Boca Raton Historical Society, but more importantly, walk the streets, visit the shops, and have lunch or dinner at one of its many fantastic restaurants to get some first-hand flavor of that town's beautiful surroundings.

Near the end of Boca Raton, we came to the Camino Real Bridge (number nineteen of twenty-seven) at mile marker 1048.2, a bascule bridge with an odd schedule: twenty minutes past the hour and forty minutes past the hour, but hey, it worked for us and it made it easy! Almost there!

A short 1.5 nautical miles later, we came to another bridge! It was amazing how many bridges were so close together! The Hillsboro Boulevard Bridge, at mile marker 1050.0, is a bascule that opens on the hour and half hour. A friend of mine warned that the bridge tender's house is around the bend, and the bridge will open only if the tender can see you. Therefore, we slowed down until we thought he spotted us. We called him on VHF channel 9 and waved as we came close, and it worked—lucky us! Abracadabra—it opened!

We traveled 4.5 nautical miles from the Hillsboro Boulevard

Bridge and reached a slight curve in the ICW to the west, for 0.2 nautical miles, at the Hillsboro Inlet. Charter fishermen heavily travel this inlet, though it can be extremely dangerous due to shoaling that shortens the depth. High winds can turn it choppy and unsafe, so best to steer clear of this area.

After traveling approximately 0.6 nautical miles past the curve, we reached the NE 14th Street Bridge (number twenty-one of twenty-seven). With a quarter-past-the-hour and quarter-to-the-hour schedule, we arrived at an opportune time to easily adjust to the bridge tender's schedule if needed. We called on VHF channel 9 and were lucky his timepiece matched ours. It was not as difficult as we thought it would be.

Only five more bridges to go! One nautical mile past the NE 14th Street Bridge, we encountered the Atlantic Boulevard Bridge at mile marker 1056.0, another bascule on an hour- and half-hour schedule. As we approached, we called on VHF channel 9 per standard procedure and were pleasantly surprised when the bridge tender was kind enough to let us go through off-schedule. I guess automobile traffic was light that day. Wow, what a nice guy!

Commercial Boulevard Bridge was only 2.5 miles away at mile marker 1059.0. We called the bridge tender who wanted to confirm our size. After we obliged, he opened the bridge, and forward we cruised.

At that point, the bridges began to appear in short succession, one after another, each about a nautical mile apart. The next was the Oakland Park Boulevard Bridge (number twenty-four of twenty-seven) at mile marker 1060.5, which opened on a quarter- and three-quarter-hour schedule. At first, the bridge tender did not answer, and I feared we might have a problem. After another try, he gave us the go-ahead to pass through the bascule bridge, and we moved along.

A nautical mile further brought us to the beginning of Fort Lauderdale, but no celebrating for us yet—not until we were safely home! Next came the East Sunrise Boulevard Bridge/SR 838 at mile marker 1062.6, also on the quarter- and three-quarter schedule. It must have been a quiet day, and my luck must have been with me, because the bridge tender let us through about three minutes early!

Two more to go! A little over a mile south, we came to the East Las Olas Boulevard Bridge, which opened on the hour and the half hour. We had to kill a little over fifteen minutes – a delay, of course! Isn't that always the case when nearly at a desired destination? So, we called, and I chit-chatted with the bridge tender, who seemed to enjoy the conversation. I figured it had to be a stressful and lonely job. My kindness must have worked because he shaved five minutes off the wait, and we glided through. I waved him a big thanks.

One more to go! Number twenty-seven, the final bridge, was only 1.6 nautical miles away, and then we could turn toward home. The SE 17th Street Bridge, also known as the Brooks Memorial

Bridge, was just ahead. I have been in and out of this bridge many times, up and down the ICW, enjoying dinner on my boat and visiting places in the area. The bridge tender is a great guy who does a great job of managing this bridge. We turned just past the bridge and headed home. Our trip had come to an end!

For me, it always feels good coming home. We could relax and take it easy after cleaning the boat and putting the essentials away. However, if you love the sea like I do, you understand the thrill you get right from the start of planning a journey and that little bit of sadness that comes when it is over.

We have taken other trips along the Intracoastal Waterway, and traveling along this vast, beautiful stretch of the Atlantic always seems like a new adventure. We always meet new people, some of whom we try to keep in touch with afterward. We have not tired of the wonders and beauty of nature and the marine life traveling the waters alongside us. We love visiting and revisiting the marinas, towns, and cities we encounter along the way. Each holds something special or new for us with each visit.

Curiosity, that lust for knowledge, is the food that feeds our brains and hearts. The excitement and stimulation we just experienced would not soon wear off. With that in mind, we knew that with a little respite, we would soon start planning our next trip. Discovering new things and enjoying new experiences is the joy of life! The galvanizing anticipation of what a trip on my boat can bring always lingers in my brain. Every time I prepare for a new adventure, my imagination sparks. I can almost catch the glint of sun reflecting off the bow and start to smell the crisp, briny, salty smell of the ocean just thinking of exploring new phenomena and spending time on my *Sea Scape*.

OVERVIEW

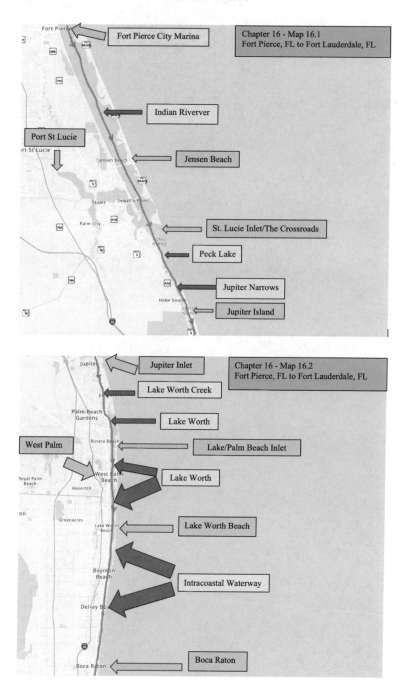

Fort Pierce City Marina

Chapter 16 - Map 16.1
Fort Pierce, FL to Fort Lauderdale, FL

Indian Riverver

Port St Lucie

Jensen Beach

St. Lucie Inlet/The Crossroads

Peck Lake

Jupiter Narrows

Jupiter Island

Jupiter Inlet

Chapter 16 - Map 16.2
Fort Pierce, FL to Fort Lauderdale, FL

Lake Worth Creek

Lake Worth

West Palm

Lake/Palm Beach Inlet

Lake Worth

Lake Worth Beach

Intracoastal Waterway

Boca Raton

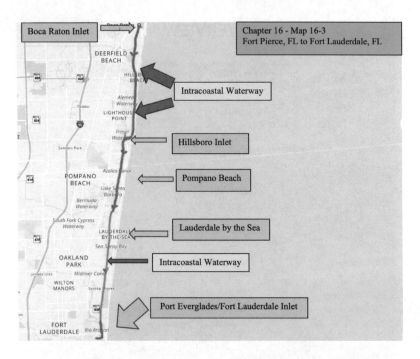

Boca Raton Inlet

Chapter 16 - Map 16-3
Fort Pierce, FL to Fort Lauderdale, FL

Intracoastal Waterway

Hillsboro Inlet

Pompano Beach

Lauderdale by the Sea

Intracoastal Waterway

Port Everglades/Fort Lauderdale Inlet

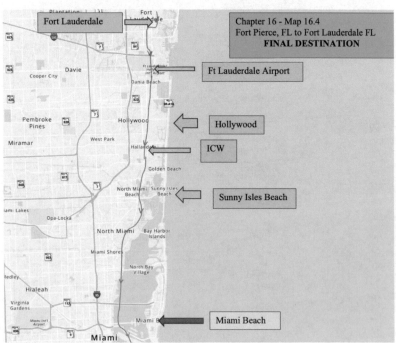

Fort Lauderdale

Chapter 16 - Map 16.4
Fort Pierce, FL to Fort Lauderdale FL
FINAL DESTINATION

Ft Lauderdale Airport

Hollywood

ICW

Sunny Isles Beach

Miami Beach

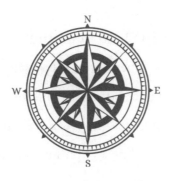

ACKNOWLEDGMENTS

Having people support your passion is indeed a blessing. I would not have been able to write this book without the help of some extraordinary people who supported my passion, desire, and vision. What you have read would have remained an empty dream without them here to help, guide, and assist me. These people have all listened, encouraged, and allowed me to pursue my passion.

First, I must give an enormous thanks to my wonderful wife, Patty. You support my passion, acknowledge my need for accomplishment, and always encourage my love of the sea. I am aware that your love and support are with me every step of the way. Every time I set out to travel up or down the Atlantic coast, your support enables my journey. Sometimes, days have turned into weeks as I've encountered problems. I know you have the strength and fortitude to handle it all. You are the most incredible wife a man could have and a wonderful mother to our children. I appreciate all you do to make our family so wonderful! Your love and support mean the world to me. Thank you, Patty, with all my heart.

A big thank you goes out to my children, Victoria, Jonathan, and Julianne, David and Jennifer. You have filled my life in more ways than you will ever know. I know you are busy with college and doing everything young adults need to do. Please follow your dreams and passions, but I also want you to know that I recognize that you allow me to follow my dreams and desires. I am eternally grateful for your support, smiles, laughter, and most importantly, your love.

My next thank you goes to Lauri Dorfman, my first mate. You are very competent, skilled, and capable in everything you do. Lauri, you have diligently served as my extra set of eyes and have always stood ready to do any job needed, whether it be cleaning filters, reading charts, helping with docking and anchoring, filling the boat with supplies, driving the boat, or providing some wholesome conversation. With your keen perception and discernment, you've helped me face some of the difficulties that come with such oceanic trips. You are a worthwhile sailor, and I might add, you prepare some excellent meals! Thank you so very much!

A special thanks goes out to Captain Mike Parks. Mike, you became our loyal and trusted travel buddy, sharing our journey with your boat, *The Matrix*. You are an accomplished captain for whom I have a great deal of respect. You know your way around a boat and its engines and have proven to be a dependable travel companion. Thank you for everything you taught me and your positive and cheerful personality.

Last but not least, an enormous thank you goes to my co-author, Cathy Wiater-Branco. This book would not have been possible without your diligence and attention to detail. I know you spent many long hours and careful thought researching and writing this book. This would not have been possible without your hard work, support, and confidence in me.

You are a special writer, a special person, and a good friend. Together, we have gained insight into the process, the details, and each other, and we make an excellent team!

REFERENCES

1. About Fort Pierce. https://www.cityoffortpierce.com/224/ About-Fort-Pierce#:~:text=Fort%20Pierce%20is%20 located%20on,watch%20on%20a%20tour%20boat. Accessed February 2023–January 2024.

2. About Norfolk. https://www.norfolk.gov/3423/About-Norfolk. Accessed February 2023–January 2024.

3. About the Breakers Palm Beach. 2024. https://www. thebreakers.com/about. Accessed February 2023–January 2024.

4. Grande Dunes. 2024. https://www.grandedunesgolf.com. Accessed February 2023–January 2024.

5. Fort Caswell. 2024. https://fortcaswell.com. Accessed February 2023–January 2024.

6. About Us. Bridge Tender Marina. 2023. https://www. bridgetendermarina.com/about. Accessed February 2023– January 2024.

7. Alligator River Marina. 2024. https://marinas.com/view/ marina/z4cnmq_Alligator_River_Marina_Columbia_NC_ United_States. Accessed February 2023–January 2024.

8. Alligator River National Wildlife Refuge Bird List. August 2009. https://www.fws.gov/sites/default/files/documents/ alligator-river-national-wildlife-refuge-bird-list.pdf. Accessed February 2023–January 2024.

9. Andrew Young Crossing, St. Augustine, Florida. January 7, 2019. http://www.atlasobscura.com/places/andrew-young-crossing Accessed February 2023–January 2024

10. Advantages and Disadvantages of Certain Types of Movable Bridges. http://theconstructor.org/structures/movable-

bridges-advantages-disadvantages/17946. Accessed February 2023–January 2024.

11. The Albemarle–Pamlico Region. https://apnep.nc.gov/our-estuary/albemarle-pamlico-region. Accessed February 2023–January 2024.

12. Alligator River Marina, Columbia, NC. https://marinas.com/view/marina/z4cnmq_Alligator_River_Marina_Columbia_NC_United_States Accessed February 2023–January 2024.

13. The Alligator River Story. https://www.oakland.edu/Assets/upload/docs/Instructor-Handbook/The-Alligator-River.Story.pdf. Accessed February 2023–January 2024.

14. Amelia Island History. 2024. http://fairbankshouse.com/amelia-island-history. Accessed February 2023–January 2024.

15. Assateague's Wild Horses. May 16, 2023. https://www.nps.gov/asis/learn-nature/horses.htm. Accessed February 2023–January 2024.

16. Navigating the Atlantic Intracoastal Waterway (AICW). 2016. https://www.atlanticintracoastalwaterway.com/navigating-the-ICW.html. Accessed February 2023–January 2024.

17. Backwater vs. Lagoon – What's the Difference? September 29, 2023. https://www.askdifference.com/backwater-vs-lagoon. Accessed February 2023–January 2024.

18. Barrier Islands. 2015–2020. https://www.scencyclopedia.org/sce/entries/barrier-islands/#:~:text=Among%20South%20Carolina's%20major%20barrier,%2C%20Hilton%20Head%2C%20and%20Daufuskie. Accessed February 2023–January 2024.

19. Beach Blog Five Reasons to Fall for the Brunswick Islands. 2024. https://www.ncbrunswick.com/blog/post/five-reasons-to-fall-for-the-brunswick-islands/Explore NC

Brunswick Islands. Accessed February 2023–January 2024.

20. A Beach Vacation with an Air of Nostalgia. 2024. https://www.ncbrunswick.com/islands-towns/oak-island Full Service Marina. http://harborgatemarinaclub.com/marina. Accessed February 2023–January 2024

21. The Best Places to See Wild Horses in North America. September 17, 2015. https://www.smithsonianmag.com/travel/best-places-see-wild-horses-north-america-180956363. Accessed February 2023–January 2024.

22. Big Talbot Island State Park. 2024. http://www.floridastateparks.org/parks-and-trails/big-talbot-island-state-park. Accessed February 2023–January 2024.

23. Blackbeard, English Pirate. https://www.britannica.com/biography/Blackbeard. Accessed February 2023–January 2024.

24. Blackbeard Island. March 28, 2017. New Georgia Encyclopedia. Accessed February 2023–January 2024.

25. Go South! Savannah. 2024. Blackbeard Island, Georgia. gosouthsavannah.com. Accessed February 2023–January 2024.

26. Looking for a New Home for Your Boat? 2024. https://www.bluepointsmarina.com. Accessed February 2023–January 2024.

27. Boating in North Carolina's Legendary Pamlico Sound. May 26, 2020. https://www.boatblurb.com/post/boating-in-north-carolina-s-legendary-pamlico-sound. Accessed February 2023–January 2024.

28. Brevard History: Haulover Canal among the Most Historic Sites on Merritt Island, Used as Early as 1606 by Indians, Explorers. August 7, 2023. http://spacecoastdaily.com/2023/10/brevard-history-haulover-canal-among-most-historic-sites-on-merritt-island-used-as-early-as-1606-by-indians-explorers. Accessed February 2023–January 2024.

29. Bridges over South Branch Elizabeth River South of Norfolk, Virginia. March 2, 2020. https://industrialscenery.blogspot. com/2020/03/bridges-over-elizabeth-river-south-of.html. Accessed February 2023–January 2024.

30. A Brief History of Williamsburg. https://williamsburgva. gov/history. Accessed February 2023–January 2024.

31. Buoyweather - Marine Forecasts. 2023. https://apps.apple. com/us/app/buoyweather-marine-forecasts/id686664992. Accessed February 2023–January 2024.

32. Indian River Lagoon Project. indianriverlagoonnews.org. Accessed February 2023–January 2024.

33. Canaveral Lock Tutorial. https://www.bing.com/videos/ riverview/relatedvideo?&q=canavaral+lock+tutorial&&mid= 849029E3673834C239B3849029E3673834C239B3&& FORM=VRDGAR. Accessed February 2023–January 2024.

34. Cape Fear. 1990–2024. https://www.imdb.com/title/ tt0101540. Accessed February 2023–January 2024.

35. Car Culture, Walter Christie. September 23, 2018. http:// www.hemmings.com/stories/article/walter-christie. Accessed February 2023–January 2024.

36. Caswell Beach. 2024. https://www.ncbrunswick.com/island-towns/casewell-beach. Accessed February 2023–January 2024.

37. Charleston Harbor Inlet. 2024. https://marinas.com/view/ inlet/9ei7dg_Charleston_Harbor_Inlet_Charleston_SC_ United_States. Accessed February 2023–January 2024.

38. Visit Norfolk. https://www.visitnorfolk.com. Accessed February 2023–January 2024.

39. Chesapeake Bay Bridge is Subject to Violent Storms. https://www.dangerousroads.org/north-america/usa/5967-chesapeake-bay-bridge.html. Accessed February 2023–January 2024.

40. Industrial Waterfront Study. https://cityofchesapeake. net/582/Industrial-Waterfront-Study. Accessed February 2023–January 2024.

41. City of Elizabeth, North Carolina. https://elizabethcitync. gov. Accessed February 2023–January 2024.

42. City of St. Augustine. 2024. http://www.visitflorida.com/ places-to-go/northeast/st-augustine. Accessed February 2023–January 2024.

43. Coastal Virginia, Hampton Roads. 2023. https://www. virginia.org/places-to-visit/regions/hampton-roads. Accessed February 2023–January 2024.

44. Common Duckweed. https://aquaplant.tamu.edu/plant-identification/alphabetical-index/duckweed/common-duckweed. Accessed February 2023–January 2024.

45. Crabby's Dockside, Fort Pierce, Florida. https:// crabbysdocksideftpierce.com. Accessed February 2023– January 2024.

46. Cruising/Navigating the AICW Norfolk, VA to Key West, FL. 2009–2023. https://www.offshoreblue.com/ cruise/aicw-intro.php; NNSY Roots; https://www. navsea.navy.mil/Home/Shipyards/Norfolk/About-Us/ History/Roots/#:~:text=The%20Norfolk%20Naval%20 Shipyard%2C%20Portsmouth,it%20was%20three%20 times%20burned. Accessed February 2023–January 2024.

47. Crystal Coast Visitors Guide. 2024. https://www. crystalcoast.com/bogue-sound.html. Accessed February 2023–January 2024.

48. Darien. 2004–2024. https://www.georgiaencyclopedia.org/ articles/counties-cities-neighborhoods/darien. Accessed February 2023–January 2024.

49. Daytona Beach, Bike Week. 2024. http://www. daytonabeach.com/bike-week. Accessed February 2023– January 2024.

50. A Deep Dive into the History of the Majestic Yacht: Ownership, Legal Disputes, and More. https://www.superyachtfan.com/yacht/majestic. Accessed February 2023–January 2024.

51. Delmarva Peninsula. https://www.britannica.com/place/Delmarva-Peninsula. Accessed February 2023–January 2024.

52. Designing Southern Cuisine for Over 30 Years. https://magnoliascharleston.com. Accessed February 2023–January 2024.

53. Destination Guides. 2024. https://www.boatsetter.com/boating-resources/category/destination-guides. Accessed February 2023–January 2024.

54. Details. 2024. http://marinas.com/view/bridge/rguqz_Crescent_Beach_Bascule_Bridge_Crescent_Beach_FL_United_States. Accessed February 2023–January 2024.

55. Did You Know These 23 Celebrities Lived in the Jupiter Area? September 2, 2021. https://www.palmbeachpost.com/story/news/local/jupiter/2021/09/02/celebrities-who-live-north-palm-beach-county-and-jupiter-area/4876894001. Accessed February 2023–January 2024.

56. Discover South Carolina. https://discoversouthcarolina.com. Accessed February 2023–January 2024.

57. Discover the 12 Coast of Florida. 2024. http://movingtofloridaguide.com/discover-the-12-coasts-of-florida.html. Accessed February 2023–January 2024.

58. Dismal Swamp Welcome Center. 2023. https://dismalswampwelcomecenter.com. Accessed February 2023–January 2024.

59. Elizabeth River Rises from the Depths. 2021. https://www.bayjournal.com/news/pollution/elizabeth-river-rises-from-the-depths/article_7abd9613-f40b-5c79-898b-faff48c1ea59.html. Accessed February 2023–January 2024.

60. Chesapeake Bay-Bridge Tunnel. https://www.cbbt.com. Accessed February 2023–January 2024.

61. Esterville Plantation – Sampit River – Georgetown County. 2019. https://south-carolina-plantations.com/georgetown/estherville.html. Accessed February 2023–January 2024.

62. Explore St. Simons Island. http://www.explorestsimonsisland.com. Accessed February 2023–January 2024.

63. Fall Bird Migration, We're Going South. 2024. https://www.visitchesapeake.com/things-to-do/birding/fall-migration. Accessed February 2023–January 2024.

64. Federal Grant to Accelerate Alligator River Bridge Project. March 10, 2023. https://coastalreview.org/2023/03/federal-grant-to-accelerate-alligator-river-bridge-project. Accessed February 2023–January 2024.

65. 15 Pros and Cons of Living on Amelia Island in Florida. 2024. http://dividendsdiversify.com/pros-cons-live-in-amelia-island-florida. Accessed February 2023–January 2024.

66. Florida Back Roads Travel. October 2, 2023. https://www.florida-backroads-travel.com/merritt-island-florida.html. Accessed February 2023–January 2024.

67. Florida: Lincolnville Historic District. http://www.nps.gov/places/florida-lincolnville-historic-district.htm. Accessed February 2023–January 2024.

68. Florida Treasure Coast https://floridastreasurecoast.com/. Accessed February 2023–January 2024.

69. Florida's Gold Coast Overview & History. 2012. https://coastal.floridanatureguide.com/gold-coast/history. Accessed February 2023–January 2024.

70. Follow the Mermaids for Fun, Food, and Entertainment! New Floating Docks and Power Now Open. 2024. https://watersidemarina.com. Accessed February 2023–January 2024.

71. Fort Lauderdale International Boat Show. 2024. https://www.flibs.com/en/home.html. Accessed February 2023–January 2024.

72. Fort Sumter. August 29, 2022. https://www.history.com/topics/american-civil-war/fort-sumter. Accessed February 2023–January 2024.

73. Georgetown Lighthouse. 2001–2024. https://lighthousefriends.com/light.asp?id=336. Accessed February 2023–January 2024.

74. Google Maps: Delaware. https://www.google.com/maps/d/viewer?mid=1yGXvRXhtm3ng1auhbaqtQOGynFw&hl=en&ll=39.15533995380491%2C-75.46575550000001&z=8. Accessed February 2023–January 2024.

75. Google Maps: Florida. https://www.google.com/search?q=google+maps+florida&sca_esv=597240485&ei=isWeZdmjH9iKptQPv5K9sAI&ved=0ahUKEwjZkPPNntODAxVYhYkEHT9JDyYQ4dUDCBA&oq=google+maps+florida&gs_lp=Egxnd3Mtd2l6LXNlcnAiE2dvb2dsZSBtYXBzIGZsb3JpZGFIAFAAWABwAHgAkAEAmAEAoAEAqgEAuAEMyAEA4gMEMEAAgQQ&sclient=gws-wiz-serp. Accessed February 2023–January 2024.

76. Google Maps: Georgia. https://www.google.com/maps/place/Georgia/@32.6507268,-85.8416216,7z/data=!3m1!4b1!4m6!3m5!1s0x88f136c51d5f8157:0x6684bc10ec4f10e7!8m2!3d32.1574351!4d-82.907123!16zL20vMGQweDg?entry=ttu. Accessed February 2023–January 2024.

77. Google Maps: Maryland. https://www.google.com/maps/place/Maryland/@39.007865,-77.6736776,7.5z/data=!4m6!3m5!1s0x89b64debe9f190df:0xf2af37657655f6b1!8m2!3d39.0457549!4d-76.6412712!16zL20vMDRycmQ?entry=ttu. Accessed February 2023–January 2024.

78. Google Maps: New Jersey. https://www.google.com/search?q=google+maps+new+jersey&sca_esv=597240485&ei=DsOeZb6iMrPk5NoPmcm5

oAQ&oq=google+maps. Accessed February 2023–January 2024.

79. Google Maps: North Carolina. https://www.google.com/maps/place/North+Carolina/@35.0547915,-85.1658515,6z/data=!3m1!4b1!4m6!3m5!1s0x88541fc4fc381a81:0xad3f30f5e922ae19!8m2!3d35.7595731!4d-79.0192997!16zL20vMDVma2Y?entry=ttu. Accessed February 2023–January 2024.

80. Google Maps: South Carolina. https://www.google.com/maps/place/South+Carolina/@33.5775198,-83.5740765,7z/data=!3m1!4b1!4m6!3m5!1s0x88f8a5697931d1e3:0xb9ffa132f505179e!8m2!3d33.836081!4d-81.1637245!16zL20vMDZ5eGQ?entry=ttu. Accessed February 2023–January 2024.

81. Google Maps: Virginia. https://www.google.com/maps/place/Virginia/@37.8842576,-84.7239784,6z/data=!3m1!4b1!4m6!3m5!1s0x884cd670bdbcb2cd:0xc04e4149b746a695!8m2!3d37.4315734!4d-78.6568942!16zL20vMDd6MW0?entry=ttu. Accessed February 2023–January 2024.

82. Great Dismal Swamp National Wildlife Refuge. https://www.fws.gov/refuge/great-dismal-swamp. Accessed February 2023–January 2024.

83. Great Egg Harbor Inlet. 2024. https://marinas.com/view/inlet/yriz9_Great_Egg_Harbor_Inlet_Longport_NJ_United_States. Accessed February 2023–January 2024.

84. Great Egg Harbor River. November 1989. https://www.rivers.gov/rivers/river/great-egg-harbor. Accessed February 2023–January 2024.

85. Grissom Parkway/Harrelson Blvd. 2024. https://www.sctrails.net/trails/trail/grissom-parkway-harrelson-blvd. Accessed February 2023–January 2024.

86. Hampton Roads, Deep Creek Lake Park. 2024. https://www.virginia.org/listing/deep-creek-lock-park/6275. Accessed February 2023–January 2024.

87. Hampton Roads – World's Greatest Harbor. 2006–2024.

https://www.hmdb.org/m.asp?m=33941. Accessed February 2023–January 2024.

88. Harborwalk Marina. https://harborwalkmarina.com. Accessed February 2023–January 2024.

89. Harbourgate Marina. Stay and Play. 2024. https://www.harbourgatemarinaclub.com. Accessed February 2023–January 2024.

90. Henry Morrison Flagler Museum, Palm Beach Florida Whitehall. 2024. https://flaglermuseum.us/history/whitehall. Accessed February 2023–January 2024.

91. Historic Columbia, NC. 2024. https://encexplorer.com/historic-columbia-nc. Accessed February 2023–January 2024.

92. Historical Overview, Our Legends and Lore Await Your Visit. https://www.wilmingtonandbeaches.com/about/area-information/historical-overview. Accessed February 2023–January 2024.

93. Jax Beach. History. http://jacksonvillebeach.org/360/History. Accessed February 2023–January 2024.

94. Jamestown Rediscovery. History. 2024. https://historicjamestowne.org/history. Accessed February 2023–January 2024.

95. Visit Beaufort. https://www.beaufortsc.org/plan-your-visit/about-the-area/history/ Accessed February 2023–January 2024.

96. The History behind the Bridge of Lions in St. Augustine. 2024. https://www.floridashistoriccoast.com/blog/the-bridge-of-lions. Accessed February 2023–January 2024.

97. History: Morehead. https://moreheadcitync.org/316/History#:~:text=Although%20most%20of%20the%20settlements,as%20Carteret%20County's%20largest%20industry. Accessed February 2023–January 2024.

98. National Park Service. Fort Matanzas. https://www.nps.gov/foma/learn/historyculture/stories.htm. Accessed February 2023–January 2024.

99. The History behind the Lions of St. Augustine. 2024. http://www.floridashistoriccoast.com/blog/the-bridge-of-lions. Accessed February 2023–January 2024.

100. History Explained: Why It's Called the Lowcountry. July 5, 2022. https://www.palmettobluff.com/discover/stories/history-explained-lowcountry. Accessed February 2023–January 2024.

101. History, Food & More, Visit Georgetown, SC. 2023. https://discovergeorgetownsc.com. Accessed February 2023–January 2024

102. History Fort Lauderdale. 2023.https://historyfortlauderdale.org/?gad_source=1&gclid=EAIaIQobChMIiqvY3tnJgwMVvExHAR3qrA5QEAAYASAAEgJvwfD_BwE. Accessed February 2023–January 2024.

103. History of Amelia Island. http://www.exploreamelia.com/Amelia_Island_History.shtml. Accessed February 2023–January 2024.

104. A History of Haulover Canal. November 5. 2017. http://nbbd.com/godo/history/Haulover-Canal/index.html. Accessed February 2023–January 2024.

105. Homes for Sale in Palm Valley, FL with waterfront. 1995–2024. http://www.realtor.com/realestateandhomes-search/Palm-Valley_FL/with_waterfront. Accessed February 2023–January 2024.

106. How St. Augustine Became the First Permanent European Settlement in America. August 29, 2023. https://www.history.com/news/st-augustine-first-american-settlement Accessed February 2023–January 2024.

107. How to Travel Through Hell Gate to Savannah. August 18,

2021. http://schoandjo.com/how-to-travel-through-hell-gate-to-savannah. Accessed February 2023–January 2024.

108. Hurricane Nicole. November 7-11, 2022. https://www.nhc.noaa.gov/data/tcr/AL172022_Nicole.pdf. Accessed February 2023–January 2024.

109. Jekyll Island. 2004–2024. http://www.georgiaencyclopedia.org/articles/geography-environment/jekyll-island. Accessed February 2023–January 2024.

110. Jekyll Island History. 2023. https://www.jekyllisland.com/history. Accessed February 2023–January 2024.

111. John Motley Morehead (1796-1866). 2016. https://northcarolinahistory.org/encyclopedia/john-motley-morehead-1796-1866. Accessed February 2023–January 2024.

112. Johnny Depp Has A New Tattoo on His Arm: Where Did He Get? https://www.marca.com/en/lifestyle/celebrities/2022/07/02/62c072d2ca4741bb3e8b45c2.html. Chincoteague Island, Virginia. https://www.chincoteague.com. Accessed February 2023–January 2024.

113. Juan Ponce de Leon. June 6, 2023. http://www.history.com/topics/exploration/juan-ponce-de-leon. Accessed February 2023–January 2024.

114. Lake Worth Inlet. 2024. https://marinas.com/view/inlet/yriy9_Lake_Worth_Inlet_Lake_Worth_FL_United_States; Coco Beach Florida, 2019. https://www.cocoabeach.com. Accessed February 2023–January 2024.

115. Little Cumberland Island. http:sherpaguides.com/georgia/coast/southern_coast/little_cumberland_island.html. Accessed February 2023–January 2024.

116. Little Cumberland Island, A Georgia Barrier Island. 2023. https://www.georgiaencyclopedia.org/articles/geography-environment/cumberland-island/. Accessed February 2023–January 2024.

117. St. Simons Island. July 20, 2017. https://www.georgiaencyclopedia.org/articles/geography-environment/st-simons-island. Accessed February 2023–January 2024.

118. Little St. Simons Island. 2024. http://www.exploregeorgia.org/city/little-st-simons-island. Accessed February 2023–January 2024.

119. Little Tiger Island, One of five Land Conservation Acquisitions in Florida. January 2023. https://www.georgiaencyclopedia.org/articles/geography-environment/cumberland-island/ Accessed February 2023–January 2024.

120. The Lodge on Little St. Simons Island. 2024. http://wwwlittlesaintsimonsisland.com. Accessed February 2023–January 2024.

121. The Loop. 2024. http://www.daytonabeach.com/biketoberfest/top-rides/the-loop. Accessed February 2023–January 2024.

122. Kaminski House Museum. https://www.kaminskimuseum.org. Accessed February 2023–January 2024.

123. Manatee Observation Deck. 2006-2023. http://floridahikes.com/manatee-observation-deck. Accessed February 2023–January 2024.

124. MapQuest: Delaware. https://www.mapquest.com/search/Delaware. Accessed February 2023–January 2024.

125. MapQuest: Florida. No Date. https://www.mapquest.com/search/Delaware. Accessed February 2023–January 2024.

126. MapQuest: Georgia. https://www.mapquest.com/search/Delaware. Accessed February 2023–January 2024.

127. MapQuest: Maryland. https://www.mapquest.com/search/Delaware. Accessed February 2023–January 2024.

128. MapQuest: New Jersey. https://www.mapquest.com/search/Delaware. Accessed February 2023–January 2024.

129. MapQuest: North Carolina. https://www.mapquest.com/search/Delaware. Accessed February 2023–January 2024.

130. MapQuest: South Carolina. https://www.mapquest.com/search/Delaware. Accessed February 2023–January 2024.

131. MapQuest: Virginia. https://www.mapquest.com/search/Delaware. Accessed February 2023–January 2024.

132. Marine Corps Base Camp Lejeune. 2024. https://www.lejeune.marines.mil. Accessed February 2023–January 2024.

133. MapQuest: Delaware. https://www.mapquest.com/search/Delaware. Accessed February 2023–January 2024.

134. MapQuest: Delaware. https://www.mapquest.com/search/Delaware. Accessed February 2023–January 2024.

135. MapQuest: Delaware. https://www.mapquest.com/search/Delaware. Accessed February 2023–January 2024.

136. Marine Corps Recruit Depot Parris Island. 2024. https://www.mcrdpi.marines.mil. Accessed February 2023–January 2024.

137. Marsh. 1996–2024. http://education.nationalgeographic.org/marsh. Accessed February 2023–January 2024.

138. Masonboro Island Reserve. https://www.deq.nc.gov/about/divisions/coastal-management/nc-coastal-reserve/reserve-sites/masonboro-island-reserve. Accessed February 2023–January 2024.

139. Merritt Island. 2024. http://www.visitflorida.com/places-to-go/central-east/merritt-island. Accessed February 2023–January 2024.

140. Morehead City Historic District. 1997–2024. https://www.livingplaces.com/NC/Carteret_County/Town_of_Morehead_City/Morehead_City_Historic_District.html. Accessed February 2023–January 2024.

141. Morehead City, North Carolina. https://moreheadcitync.org/314/Docking-Facilities. Accessed February 2023–January 2024.

142. Mosquito Lagoon Aquatic Preserve. 2024. https://floridadep.gov/rcp/aquatic-preserve/locations/mosquito-lagoon-aquatic-preserve. Accessed February 2023–January 2024.

143. What Does Redfish Taste Like? August 29, 2022. http://www.alices.kitchen/fish-or-seafood/redfish-taste. Accessed February 2023–January 2024.

144. Myrtle Beach and the Grand Strand – A Vacation Mecca. 2024. https://discoversouthcarolina.com/articles/myrtle-beach-and-the-grand-strand-a-vacation-mecca. Accessed February 2023–January 2024.

145. Naval Submarine Base Kings Bay. August 17, 2023. http://installations.militaryonesource.mil/in-depth-overview/naval-submarine-base-kings-bay. Accessed February 2023–January 2024.

146. Navionics Boating App. 2023. https://www.navionics.com/usa. Accessed February 2023–January 2024.

147. Norfolk History. 2024. https://www.city-data.com/us-cities/The-South/Norfolk-History.html. Accessed February 2023–January 2024.

148. Naval Sea Systems Command. https://www.navsea.navy.mil/Home/Shipyards/Norfolk. Accessed February 2023–January 2024.

149. The North Carolina Seafood Festival. 2024. https://www.ncseafoodfestival.org. Accessed February 2023–January 2024.

150. Oak Island Map. https://oak-islandnc.com/oak-island-map. Accessed February 2023–January 2024.

151. Onslow Swing Bridge to Be Replaced Due to Age, Maintenance Costs. February 16, 2022. https://www.publicradioeast.org/2022-02-16/onslow-swing-bridge-to-be-replaced-due-to-age-maintenance-costs. Accessed February 2023–January 2024.

152. Paddling with Dolphins in the Intracoastal Waterway. 2024. https://wildernessclassroom.org/paddling-with-dolphins-in-the-intracoastal-waterway. Accessed February 2023–January 2024.

153. "The Palm Coast Historian" Archives. 2024. https://palmcoasthistory.org/historiansnewsletters. Accessed February 2023–January 2024.

154. Palm Coast History Brief. 2024. http://www.palmcoast.gov/historical-society. Accessed February 2023–January 2024.

155. Pamlico Sound. 2024. https://www.outerbanks.com/pamlico-sound.html. Accessed February 2023–January 2024.

156. Paradise Creek Nature Park. 2024. https://dwr.virginia.gov/vbwt/sites/paradise-creek-nature-park. Accessed February 2023–January 2024.

157. Pasquotank County (1668). 2016. https://northcarolinahistory.org/encyclopedia/pasquotank-county-1668. Accessed February 2023–January 2024.

158. Pasquotank River Basin. https://files.nc.gov/deqee/documents/files/pasquotank.pdf. Accessed February 2023–January 2024.

159. Pasquotank River Basin Documents. https://www.deq.nc.gov/about/divisions/mitigation-services/dms-planning/watershed-planning-documents/pasquotank-river-basin-documents. Accessed February 2023–January 2024.

160. Navigating the Atlantic Intracoastal Waterway (AICW). https://www.atlanticintracoastalwaterway.com/navigating-the-ICW.html. Accessed February 2023–January 2024.

161. Port Canaveral. History. https://www.portcanaveral.com/About/History. Accessed February 2023–2024.

162. Portside Marina. https://www.portsidemarina.com. Accessed February 2023–January 2024.

163. The Spirit of Florida. http://www.staugustinedistillery.com. Accessed February 2023–January 2024.

164. BoatUS. 2024. https://www.boatus.com. Accessed February 2023–January 2024.

165. The Queen of the Carolina Sea Islands. 2023. https://rhetthouseinn.com/beaufort-history. Accessed February 2023–January 2024.

166. Race of the Gentlemen: See the Rides, Meet People Keeping Pre-1950s Racing Alive. July 5, 2017. https://www.rollingstone.com/culture/culture-lists/race-of-gentlemen-see-the-rides-meet-people-keeping-pre-1950's-racing-alive-196864. Accessed February 2023–January 2024.

167. The Race of the Gentlemen Celebrates 10 Years of the Finest Automotive Beach Racing in the World. July 22, 2022. https://www.prnewswire.com/news-releases/the-race-of-gentlemen-celebrates-ten-years-of-the-finest-automotive-beach-racing-in-the-world-301591798.html. Accessed February 2023–January 2024.

168. Rayleigh scattering. http://www.britannica.com/science/Rayleigh-scattering. Accessed February 2023–January 2024.

169. A Record-Breaking Number of Loggerhead Sea Turtle Nests on Masonboro Island. October 6, 2022. https://www.whqr.org/local/2022-10-06/a-record-breaking-number-of-loggerhead-sea-turtle-nests-on-Masonboro-island. Accessed February 2023–January 2024.

170. Reed. http://www.britannica.com/plant/reed-plant. Accessed February 2023–January 2024.

171. Remember When You Could Drive on the Beach? 2024. https://www.visitjacksonville.com/about/research-information/history. Accessed February 2023–January 2024.

172. Replacing Bascule Bridge Set Off a Mighty Struggle. January 19, 2017. http://www.caller.com/story/news/columnists/murphy-givens/2017/01/19/givens-replacing-bascule-bridge-set-off-mighty-struggle/96767716. Accessed February 2023–January 2024.

173. Georgia Department of Natural Resources Division. Gastateparks.org. Accessed February 2023–January 2024.

174. Ripley Light Yacht Club. https://ripleylightyachtclub.com. Accessed February 2023–January 2024.

175. River Restoration in Virginia. https://intersector.com/case/ elizabethriver_virginia. Accessed February 2023–January 2024.

176. Robert N. Reed, Sr. Downtown Waterfront Park. 2024. https://marinas.com/view/marina/7ecqj5j_Robert_N_ Reed_Sr_Downtown_Waterfront_Park_Chincoteague_VA_ United_States. Accessed February 2023–January 2024.

177. Route 52 Causeway Bridge Replacement, Somers Point and Ocean City. October 16, 2013. https://www.nj.gov/ transportation/commuter/roads/route52. Accessed February 2023–January 2024.

178. Sabal Palmetto. https://plants.ces.ncsu.edu/plants/sabal- palmetto. Accessed February 2023–January 2024.

179. Safe Harbor Port Royal. https://shmarinas.com/locations/ safe-harbor-port-royal. Accessed February 2023–January 2024.

180. 7 Reasons Why Fort Lauderdale is the Yacht Capital of the World. December 28, 2022. https://www.boatsetter.com/ boating-resources/fort-lauderdale-the-yacht-capital-of-the- world. Accessed February 2023–January 2024.

181. Sailing Distance Calculator. 2024. https://www.bednblue. com/sailing-distance-calculator. Accessed February 2023– January 2024.

182. Saint Augustine Historic District. 2024. http://www. floridashistoriccoast.com/things-to-do/history/historic- district. Accessed February 2023–January 2024.

183. Visit St Augustine, Historical Sites. 2003–2024. https:// www.visitstaugustine.com/things-to-do/historic-sites.

Accessed February 2023–January 2024.

184. Saint Lucie Inlet State Park. http://www.stateparks.com/saint_lucie_inlet_state_park_in_florida.html. Accessed February 2023–January 2024.

185. San Miguel de Guadalupe. https://www.britannica.com/place/San-Miguel-de-Guadalupe. Accessed February 2023–January 2024.

186. Sapelo Island. https://georgiawildlife.com/sapelo-island-wma. Accessed February 2023–January 2024.

187. South Carolina Counties Investing in Workforce Development. November 30, 2023. https://www.richmondfed.org/press_room/our_news/2023/20231130_community_conversation_sc. Accessed February 2023–January 2024.

188. St. Augustine Inlet. 2024. http://marinas.com/view/inlet/rqinp_St_Augustine_Inlet_St_Augustine_FL_United_States. Accessed February 2023–January 2024.

189. Stay at Your Own Private Island, Swansboro, NC. 2021. https://the-travel-life.com/stay-at-your-own-private-island-swansboro-nc. Accessed February 2023–January 2024.

190. The Story of Lincolnville. 2024. http://www.floridashistoriccoast.com/blog/the-story-of-lincolnville. Accessed February 2023–January 2024.

191. Sullivan's Island Was the African American Ellis Island. 2009. https://www.nationalparkstraveler.org/2009/03/sullivan-s-island-african-american-ellis-island. Accessed February 2023–January 2024.

192. A Taste of Georgetown's History. 2009–2019. https://www.historicgeorgetownsc.com/history. Accessed February 2023–January 2024.

193. The Timucua, North Florida's Early People. http://www.nps.gov/timu/learn/historyculture/timupeople.htm.

Accessed February 2023–January 2024.

194. 10 Sailing & Boating Superstitions. 2023. https://www. discoverboating.com/resources/boating-and-sailing-superstitions. Accessed February 2023–January 2024.

195. Top Ten Rules for Marina Etiquette. March 7, 2013. https:// www.boatingmag.com/top-ten-rules-marina-etiquette. Accessed February 2023–January 2024.

196. TROG, The Race of Gentlemen. 2023. https://www. theraceofgentlemen.com. Accessed February 2023–January 2024.

197. Tropical Depression Nicole Moves through Georgia. November 11, 2022. https://www.carolinacoastonline.com/ regional/article_b052f4f0-61bc-11ed-9ba1-9fc772a231f7. html. Accessed February 2023–January 2024.

198. Tuckahoe River. 2024. https://www.touristlink.com/united-states/tuckahoe-river-new-jersey/overview.html. Accessed February 2023–January 2024.

199. How to Stay Safe from 13 Sailor Superstitions. September 21, 2023. https://www.boaterexam.com/blog/boater-superstitions. Accessed February 2023–January 2024.

200. Village of Deep Creek, the Dismal Swamp Rangers. https:// www.cityofchesapeake.net/DocumentCenter/View/4670/ Village-of-Deep-Creek-PDF. Accessed February 2023–January 2024.

201. Wallops Flight Facility. December 20, 2023. https://www. nasa.gov/wallops. Accessed February 2023–January 2024.

202. Waterside Marina. 2024. https://watersidemarina.com. Accessed February 2023–January 2024.

203. Waterway Guide. 2024. https://www.waterwayguide.com. Accessed February 2023–January 2024.

204. Welcome to Bike Week. 2023. https://officialbikeweek.com. Accessed February 2023–January 2024.

205. Welcome to the Bridge Tender Marina. 2023. https://www. bridgetendermarina.com. Accessed February 2023–January 2024.

206. Welcome to Chesapeake. 2024. https://www.visitchesapeake. com. Accessed February 2023–January 2024.

207. Welcome to Chincoteague Island, VA. https://www. chincoteague.com. Accessed February 2023–January 2024.

208. Welcome to the Frances Marion and Sumter National Forests. https://www.fs.usda.gov/scnfs. Accessed February 2023–January 2024.

209. Welcome to Isle of Palms, South Carolina's Unique Coastal Barrier Island. https://www.isleofpalmsexplorer.com. Accessed February 2023–January 2024.

210. Welcome to the Golden Islands. 2024. https://www. goldenisles.com. Accessed February 2023–January 2024.

211. Welcome to the GTM Research Reserve! 2023. http:// gtmnerr.org. Accessed February 2023–January 2024

212. Welcome to the Oak Island Lighthouse. 2024. https://www. oakislandlighthouse.org. Accessed February 2023–January 2024.

213. Welcome to the Rice Museum. 2023. https://www. ricemuseum.org. Accessed February 2023–January 2024.

214. Welcome to the Treasure Coast. https://www.visittreasure. com. Accessed February 2023–January 2024.

215. Welcome to The Treasure Coast. https:// floridastreasurecoast.com. Accessed February 2023–January 2024.

216. What Are the Advantages and Disadvantages for a Fixed VS Movable Bridge For Urban Traffic? 2024. http://www. linkedin.com/advice/0/what-advantages-disadvantages-fixed-vs-movable. Accessed February 2023–January 2024.

217. 5 Pink Sky Spiritual Meanings. http://ententechicago.com/what-does-it-mean-when-the-sky-is-pink. Accessed February 2023–January 2024.

218. What is the Carolina Lowcountry? November 14, 2022. https://www.southernliving.com/travel/south-carolina/why-its-called-lowcountry. Accessed February 2023–January 2024.

219. What You Need to Know About Slavery and Sullivan's Island. July 9, 2021. https://blackthen.com/what-you-need-to-know-about-slavery-and-sullivans-island. Accessed February 2023–January 2024.

220. Where Do Dates (fruit) Come From? May 19, 2013. https://wanttoknowit.com/where-do-dates-fruit-come-from. Accessed February 2023–January 2024.

221. Our History. 2024. http://www.bocahistory.org/our-history. Accessed February 2023–January 2024.

222. Why Do We Call It . . . Hampton Roads? February 3, 2022. https://wydaily.com/our-community/2022/02/03/why-do-we-call-it-hampton-roads. Accessed February 2023–January 2024.

223. Windward Beach Marina. https://mywindward.com/windward-beach-marine. Accessed February 2023–January 2024.

224. Winyah Bay Station. 2024. https://northinlet.sc.edu/winyah-bay-station. Accessed February 2023–January 2024.

225. America's Parks. stateparks.com. Accessed February 2023–January 2024.

226. World Temperatures – Weather Around the World. 1995–2024. https://www.timeanddate.com/weather. Accessed February 2023–January 2024.

227. Worldwide Wind and Weather Forecasts. 2023. https://www.windfinder.com/forecast. Accessed February 2023–January 2024.

228. Wrightsville Beach Bridge. 2024. https://www.starnewsonline.com/story/business/transportation/2019/05/21/wrightsville-beach-gets-first-look-at-drawbridge-replacement-options/5091251007. Accessed February 2023–January 2024.

229. Your Gateway to the Wild. 2023. https://dismalswampwelcomecenter.com. Accessed February 2023–January 2024.

230. Explore Florida's Space Coast. 2024. https://www.visitspacecoast.com. Accessed February 2023–January 2024

231. Yank Marina, New Jersey's Only Commercial Shipbuilder. 2023. https://yankmarine.com. Accessed February 2023–January 2024.

232. Yorktown, Historic Town, Virginia, United States. December 29, 2023. https://www.britannica.com/place/Yorktown-historical-Virginia. Accessed February 2023–January 2024.

RAMI GEFFNER

Captain Rami Geffner, MD's strong affinity and fondness for the ocean has been a steadfast presence throughout his life. From an early age, Rami accompanied his father on a number of sailing trips, where he fell in love with everything about the sea. He now plans and sets out on his own seafaring adventures and is involved with the local maritime community. Rami holds a bachelor's degree in biology, a master's in human anatomy from Rutgers University, a medical degree from the New Jersey School of Medicine, and as well as multiple degrees in Derma Pathology. Pursuing a career in the medical field, Rami set up a multitude of dermatology practices in New Jersey to provide life-saving procedures. He lives with his wife in the majestic Barnegat Bay area, where he manages a fleet of boats. This is his first book.

CATHERINE WIATER-BRANCO

C.W. Branco is a well-decorated educator with forty-six years of experience in teaching, leading and mentoring. Cathy pursued a degree in education at the University of Bridgeport, and a master's from Seton Hall University. After teaching in the classroom for several years, she, along with a few selected teachers, was invited to join the Instructional Theory into Practice program of her school district. From there she held many other noted education positions including work at Kean University. She has always had a strong affinity towards the teaching of literacy, especially writing. After a long and varied career, Cathy retired and now spends her free time writing and painting. She resides in Western Monmouth County, New Jersey with her husband and not far from her beautiful daughter.

Made in the USA
Columbia, SC
04 November 2024

45150555R00191